ALPHA BITCH
to
ENCHANTRESS

A Path to Awaken Your Feminine Superpowers

Suki Sohn

Published by Best Seller Publishing®, Pasadena, CA
Best Seller Publishing® is a registered trademark
Printed in the United States of America.

ISBN: 978-1-946978-90-5

DISCLAIMER

Cover Design: Jennifer Stimson
Editing: Bethany Davis
Author Photo Credit: Elena Kosharny

Table of Contents

The union of masculine and feminine energies is key to our ultimate spiritual freedom. Without the male or female aspect, there is no enlightenment: there is no union of wisdom and method; there is no union of clear light and illusion body; there is no union of mind and body.

– Gehlek Rinpoche

Dedications

To my teacher of the Divine Feminine Path,
Lama Tsultrim Allione.

To my husband John and beautiful two boys
Jake and Jaden, who have been
my constant source of inspiration and joy.

Foreword

I met Suki at my retreat center Tara Mandala and learned
that she was writing a book to help women awaken and
cultivate empowered femininity in their lives. She was there
to gain clarity and insight to complete her book. I was happy
to hear this as I recognized in her a 'woman rising' to the call
of the Great Mother. I also share her passion for this mission.
To aid her in her journey as a messenger, when she asked to
take refuge with me, I gave her the spiritual name of Choying
Khandro (or Dakini of the Dharmadhatu), which translates
As 'Dakini (female wisdom holder) of Basic Space'.

The whisper of the Great Mother is spreading and
growing louder. Recent social movements are just the
beginning of the much-needed change in the world to honor
and embrace the wisdom of the feminine. Fear, which is
the basis for all negative mental and emotional afflictions,

comes from a rupture, a split from the infinite source of all life, the ground of being, the Great Mother.

In this book, Suki introduces key feminine qualities, how they apply to your daily life, and how to cultivate them. She adeptly integrates many different spiritual traditions and science to present a holistic and practical view of the empowered feminine to heal this rupture. This book will help awaken the innate wisdom of the feminine in you and show you how to integrate it into your life. I am delighted to have been part of her journey and believe that your lives will be enriched by insights Suki has shared in this book.

Lama Tsultrim Allione
Founder of Tara Mandala
Author of *Women of Wisdom and Feeding Your Demons*
Recognized as reincarnation of renowned 11th Century
Tibetan Yogini Machig Labdron
(founder of the Mother Lineage in Tantric Buddhism)

Author's Note

If you do not believe that humans are capable of developing or awakening to supernatural abilities then stop right here, put this book down, and walk away. This book isn't for those looking for mundane and tactical dating advice such as *how to get a guy to commit* or *how to improve your social dating profile,* but those who seek a more enchanted life. This book is about shapeshifting, magic, and embracing the depth of mysteries that are inherent to the feminine path. Who this book *is* for are those who by genuine curiosity, some serendipitous miracle, a personal tragedy, or unexpected personal breakthrough were able peer behind the veil to witness the mysteries of life.

This book is a coming out of sorts for me. I held back my truth and the entirety of my journey in fear of judgment and isolation, yet this fear started to erode my hard-earned supernatural abilities, or what I call feminine superpowers, as my brain continued to doubt my newly-acquired powers. Validation at all levels is such an important part of any kind of growth – the most important being the validation one offers oneself.

Because I was conscious of my community and an audience who did not believe in metaphysical influences in our daily lives, I attempted to use the latest scientific findings to support my ideas in order to appease my more skeptical audiences. However, I now realize that this effort is really futile. For those ready to peer behind the veil, ideas I share will feel like a remembrance. Science is only just catching up to what the spiritual adepts have known for millennia.

Over a decade ago, I started to have experiences I could not explain with logic. I started having vivid visions of my past lives so real that I could feel the emotions that these other versions of me felt in their lives. In a moment's ecstatic trance, I shapeshifted into a black jaguar. I talked to trees and could feel their different personalities. I could not share these experiences with my friends at the time, as they probably would think I had gone nuts. Fortunately, I was able to meet a number of people along the way who had once lived a corporate lifestyle and had become awakened to a different understanding of the world.

Many of them encouraged me to speak my truth and step firmly into my role as the healer and guide that I am and have been for many lifetimes. Though I may risk ridicule, at least I won't be burnt alive in this lifetime for my beliefs and abilities! How could I possibly guide my clients toward empowerment if I could not proudly embrace all that I am?

The Other World is seductive, and it is very easy to get lost in it. Once you have tasted the spiritual ecstasy and peace available to you in the Other World, this physical three-dimensional world can feel heavy, oppressive, and boring. However, we are here in our physical bodies because we have work to do and there is no escaping that. The more you try to run from the work you need to do, the more painful the lesson will be. So, embrace the challenges life offers because there is no getting around it. At one point or another you will have to face the lessons your soul yearns to learn and the wisdom the Universe wants to provide. Once you completely accept this you will be able to see all life experiences as sacred.

Lama Tsultrim says, *"The loss of feminine qualities is an urgent psychological and ecological issue in modern society. It is a painful loss in our emotional lives and a disastrous loss for the safety of life on earth."*

In sharing her vision, this book at its core is about reclaiming a feminine legacy of humanity once connected to nature, Earth, the Great Mother that was lost with industrial civilization, and also to serve as a guided journey to rebalance the masculine and feminine within us all.

Introduction

If you picked up this book, you are perhaps looking for guidance on how to improve your love life. You will certainly get that, but my aim is that you will walk away with much more. My aim is not simply to improve your love life, but for you to embody and awaken the divine feminine in you.

This book is about finding, nurturing, and expanding your capacity for love. It is not a book focused on tactical advice but rather a journey of self-transformation that allows you to emerge radiant and magnetic.

Any good personal trainer or weight loss expert will tell you that toning and slimming down only one part of your body is not possible unless you are getting liposuction. The body is a holistic system that works together and any work you do in one area will have impact on other parts of your body.

Your mind and heart, your love, career, and health work the same way. Learning how to remove love blocks is not an endeavor that is or can be isolated to only that aspect of your life. The feedback and patterns you have established in other parts of your life inevitably impact your beliefs and behaviors around love.

I choose to start my work with my clients on relationships because this is the area where my clients are willing to go deep fast. Working with numerous women I realized that at the core most of, if not all of, their challenges were the lack of a model for empowered femininity.

I will confess right up front that I have an agenda. An agenda for my clients, our society, and the world. That agenda is to help bring back divine and empowered femininity. It is high time to embrace the innate feminine qualities that have been degraded, marginalized, and suppressed for centuries.

When I was a teenager, a close family friend was hospitalized when she was five months pregnant because she was beaten by her husband. Her husband, the baby's father, kicked her so hard in the face that it ripped her mouth open to the middle of her cheek. When her mother-in-law came to visit, shockingly she said, "What did you do to make my son so mad?"

Our friend ended up losing the baby and they got divorced. But that woman's comment stuck in my head. I realized that mothers like her are creating these violent and abusive men, either from blind coddling, poor parenting, or by neglect and lack of nurturing. I realized that we as women need to become empowered within to see real change in the world. More women in more power positions will not necessarily lead to healing humanity, but more women who embody and model empowered feminine values to their children, colleagues, lovers, and society will.

There is certainly work to be done, so I am counting on the alpha bitches of this world to fully recognize the power of femininity and honor their innate feminine qualities. If we as women do not honor our femininity, the essence of who we are, how can we expect a man to? We are the ones we have been waiting for. We need to become the change we would like to see.

This book is a manual for empowered femininity. Throughout the following chapters we will explore:

- Historical perspectives and definitions of femininity in various spiritual traditions and cultures

- The impact of the loss of empowered femininity in the world and in our lives

- Defining empowered femininity in the modern world and why you should embrace these qualities

- And finally, how to cultivate these feminine super-powers so you can have the love and life you want!

CHAPTER 1

Defining Femininity

Truth about Eve

Many people are unaware that Eve was Adam's second wife. According to the Babylonian Talmud, written 3–5 BCE, prior to Eve, Adam had a wife named Lilith. Just like Adam, she was made of earth and brought to life with the breath of God. In other words, she was cut of the same cloth as Adam. However, the union was short-lived, as Lilith wanted to "be on top" and did not want to yield authority to Adam.

Lilith left Adam after she refused to become subservient to him, and then would not return to the Garden of Eden after she had coupled with the archangel Samael, the angel of death and the taker of souls. From this point, the

Abrahamic religious scholars demonized Lilith and she was portrayed as a dangerous monster of the night, a sexually wanton woman seducing men to their peril.

The story of Eve and Lilith can be seen as yet another example of the patriarchal church's attempt to subjugate women. Feminists would view Lilith's departure from Eden as an act of triumph and self-empowerment. This may be so, but there is a deeper meaning to this story than what meets the eye.

Eve and Lilith represent the dual aspects of femininity. Lilith is Queen of the Night, just as Persephone of the Greek pantheon, Ereshkigal of the Sumerians, Kali of the Hindus, Nut of the Egyptians, and the fierce Dakinis of Tantric Buddhism. She is the gatekeeper to the mysteries, death, and everything that lurks in the dark of the night. She is the wild untamed and unfathomable feminine that cannot be controlled or subjugated. She is the ultimate alpha bitch.

Eve, on the other hand, is in the form of the consort of man. Eve was made of something secret, hidden, and not visible to the eye, Adam's rib. The creation of Eve alludes to the enchanting, gentle, subtle, and alluring aspect of the feminine. It also describes another Law of Nature, the need for polarity for attraction and harmony. Lilith and Adam were of the positive pole, the emanating aspect, while Eve is of the negative pole, the receiving aspect of nature. Lilith and Adam's identical positive polarity caused them to repel each other.

In order for a woman to become whole and empowered, she must embrace both the Lilith and Eve aspects within her. Lilith as the "room of her own," the fierce and primal force, and Eve the harmonious subtle aspect. Feminists who champion Lilith and reject their Eve aspect will often find themselves alone and isolated, and women who reject the Lilith aspect will find themselves submissive and defenseless.

In Taoist philosophy, the Feminine, the Yin is mysterious, subtle, and invisible. However, this does not make her any less powerful. The physical and apparent aspect of the Universe is Yang, while the metaphysical and unapparent is the realm of the Yin. Scientists have long known that our bodies are more empty space than physical matter. Atomic matter is what we perceive as the reality around us. In truth, it constitutes only 4% of the universe, while what we perceive as "empty space" is filled with what physicists call dark matter and dark energy, the Yin. In this sense, the Taoist view of Yin incorporates the dual aspect of Lilith and Eve, the powerful and yielding aspects of the Feminine. Gender does not define these dual aspects of nature nor are these dual aspects actually distinct from each other. In the Taoist symbol, you will notice a white dot in the black and a black dot in the white, which demonstrates the illusion of duality as the Yang and Yin give rise to each other.

YANG		**YIN**
Masculine		Feminine
Physical		Metaphysical
Sun		Moon
Day		Night
Bold		Subtle
Visible		Invisible
Rising		Descending
Fast		Slow
Atomic Matter		Dark Matter & Dark Energy

The true lesson behind the story of Lilith, Adam, and Eve is about relating to the opposite sex and that harmony, union, and procreation were possible between Adam and Eve because they were different and of opposite poles. Polarity maintains attraction. This still holds true for modern relationships. Though gender is a prominent factor, it does not have to be the ultimate determinant of who in the relationship is Yang and who is Yin. There are plenty of heterosexual couples where the woman takes on a more traditionally masculine role in the relationship and the man a more supportive role. However, in coming across relationships like that, more often than not, I find a neurotic and controlling woman and an emasculated, frustrated man.

The Feminine According to Science

Now let's take a look at how science is discovering the innate qualities and natural strengths of women based on biology.

What are the differences between men and women? Do women have innate abilities that are unique and separate from men? According to science, the answer is a resounding yes. Firstly, there are structural differences in the female and male brains. The human brain is made up of grey and white matter. The grey matter acts like data processing centers while white matter functions as networks that connect the various processing centers. Neuroscientists have discovered that in the male brain grey matter is activated ten times more than in the female brain, while white matter is activated seven times more in women than men.

The difference in activation results in a masculine brain, which is more conducive to focused tunnel vision, while the female brain lends itself to a wider perspective, both physically and emotionally, that allows them to better contextualize and connect ideas. The developed white matter in women allows them to have relatively more advanced abilities in language and communication as well as connect emotions to thoughts and actions.

Hormonally, it is well known that testosterone influences muscular development, libido, and levels of aggression in men. In women, higher levels of oxytocin, also known as the "love hormone," encourage women to seek intimate connection.[1]

Based on structural and hormonal differences, it is clear that each has its own set of strengths and weaknesses. The masculine lends itself to an active and dynamic force that seeks and even thrives in competition, while the feminine is prone to avoiding conflict and seeking connection and harmony. In Chapter 4, we will explore these concepts and their manifestation in daily life in more detail.

The Feminine in Spirituality

In spiritual traditions across the world, the feminine is imbued with creative power and is the true agent of all change.

In Vedic tradition, the feminine element is known as *Shakti,* a source of creativity and fertility, cosmic existence and liberation, which in our bodies manifests as the kundalini, a psycho-spiritual force residing at the base of our spine. The ascension of kundalini energy up the spine through the chakras, energy centers of the body, is considered a phenomenon of enlightenment.

Taoists called the "outwardly" passive female principle of the Universe Yin. Yet the Yin is the sustaining force of life, and is associated with earth, water, moon, and the night. It is dark, obscure, cold, slow, soft, yielding, diffuse, magnetic, and mysterious in nature.

In Hellenistic philosophy and in Christian theology, Sophia, the Greek for "wisdom," was considered an expression of the feminine aspect in the Holy Trinity. Sophia represented the Holy Spirit, the formless aspect of the Creator. In Judaism, God is traditionally described in the masculine, but in the mystical Judaic tradition of the Kabbalah, the *Shekhinah*, which translates to "holy presence," represents the feminine aspect.

Islam may not consistently describe the role of the Divine Feminine; however, in Prophet Muhammad's defining peak experience of being elevated through the seven heavens to the realms of the Creator, he is said to have been riding a winged white horse, with a face of a woman called the "*Buraq*." The pure divine force that enabled Muhammad to elevate to supreme consciousness is feminine in nature. The flight of the Buraq resembles closely the idea of kundalini rising described in Vedic traditions.

In Tibetan Tantric Buddhist traditions, the feminine principle is embodied in the *Dakini*, which is Sanskrit for "Sky Dancer" or "Sky Goer." As embodiment of enlightenment and transcendent wisdom, Dakinis are luminous, subtle, spiritual energy, the key, and the gatekeeper.

It is apparent that throughout the world's ancient spiritual traditions, sages knew that the feminine aspect is the vehicle, as either a formless life force or as transcendent wisdom, to higher levels of consciousness and enlightenment.

Mitochondrial DNA, the Matrilineal DNA

Jumping back to science, the idea of the feminine as the ultimate sustaining life force is seen in our genetic makeup. Mitochondria are like little factories within each cell that are the energy source for your body. They make energy, or ATP (Adenosine Triphosphate), from eating and breathing. Many mind-body yogic and Taoist traditions knew the importance of diet and breath for the optimal functioning of our bodies. What is interesting is that mitochondria are inherited exclusively from the mother.

Unlike the linear, double helix DNA that is inherited from both parents, with one strand coming from your mother and the other strand from your father, Mitochondrial DNA is circular and comes only from the female. mDNA is the direct feminine lineage of humanity, as well as the power source for our bodies.

Prophecies and Legends of the Rise of the Feminine

There is an ancient prophecy of the Amazon and the high Andes that speaks of the divergence of the path of the Condor and the Eagle. The Condor represents the feminine aspect, the path of the heart, intuition, and harmony with nature. The Eagle represents the masculine, the path of the mind, logic, and control over nature.

According to this prophecy, 1490 would be the beginning of the 500-year cycle in which the path of the Eagle would reign to the point of near-extinction of the path of the Condor. 1492, the year in which Christopher Columbus landed in the Americas, marked the beginning of the end for the Native American and indigenous South American tribal traditions, which continues to this day.

Yet there is hope, as the prophecy also states that in the next 500-year period starting from 1990, there is a potential for the Condor and Eagle to come together to fly in the same sky and create a new path that unifies the two. However, the prophecy only speaks of the potential, suggesting that human choices will determine the final outcome. One thing is clear. If we continue to leave the feminine marginalized in favor of the masculine, we as individuals, our society, and our children will undoubtedly suffer the consequences.

According to the renowned Kabbalist Rabbi Isaac Luria (1534–1572), feminine values will be mirrored in the "last leg" of our history, causing and heralding the messianic era and ultimate redemption when the feminine role and qualities will be valued and appreciated. In describing the feminine and masculine, Dr. Yisroel Susskind writes:

> *Endurance and breadth are characteristic of the feminine forces, while intensity and focus are masculine. In computer terminology, parallel processing is feminine, whereas serial processing is masculine. In football, the wide receiver*

is feminine, while the quarterback is masculine. The
transcendental number pi is feminine, while logarithms are
masculine. Analog is feminine, while digital is masculine.
My favorite metaphor for the difference is that gravity is a
feminine force, while lightning is a masculine force.

[Further] the very concept of redemption is intrinsically
related to women. In Kabbalistic terms, it is explained
that the Sefira[2] of Malchut reflects the feminine
dimension. During the periods of exile, Malchut is in
a state of descent and does not receive direct influence
from the other Sefirot*. Metaphorically, this condition
is described as the feminine in an enforced state of
separation from the higher emanations of the creative
force. Conversely, in the Era of the Redemption, "a
woman of valor [will be] the crown of her husband."
The higher source of Malchut will be revealed, the direct
bond between Malchut and the other Sefirot will be
reestablished, and Malchut will become a source of vital
influence, renewing the totality of existence.[3]

Nostradamus also prophesied the rise and empowerment
of women, who will heal the world with love, compassion,
cooperation, and harmony. Manuela Dunn Mascetti and
Peter Lorie in their book *Nostradamus: Prophecies for Women*
have interpreted Nostradamus's prophecies that predict the
decline of patriarchy.[4]

New law to occupy the new land
Toward Syria, Judeau and Palestine:
The great barbarian empire of men decay,
Before the moon completes its cycle.

— *Century 3:97*

Mascetti and Lorie interprets this as:

A new law will emerge in the new world of America,
At a time when Syria, Judeau and Palestine are
significant: The great barbarian empire of
patriarchy that men have created will decay
During the time that the feminine spirit is completing
its cycle.

The modern feminist movements seem to be a poignant manifestation of the prophecies of the various spiritual traditions. However, it is important to recognize that the prophecy is about feminine qualities of creation, not women as a gender. The recent feminist movements that have galvanized and given women permission to stand up against the abuses men in power have inflicted upon them is a worthy and inspiring cause. Yet, there are some unfortunate incidents to turn this rightful cause in to a witch-hunt of men by some angry and vindictive women. This kind of aggressive, combative, and hateful attitude makes this contingent no different in nature to the oppressors they claim to oppose.

It is Time for the Soft Light of the Moon

A wolf wearing a sheepskin does not make it a sheep. Just because you are in woman's body does not mean you automatically possess the feminine qualities of redemption and enlightenment that the spiritual traditions talk about. It is true that biologically women are more likely to exhibit and possess feminine qualities. However, I have come across many women who think and behave more like men than women. In fact, I don't believe that the "redemption" of humanity and ushering in the new world order is about women but rather reclaiming and integrating feminine wisdom that industrialized humanity has all but forgotten.

Modern society at large rewards and values masculine traits – mental abilities or emotional connection; logic over intuition; competition over collaboration. As such, women started to lose touch with their femininity and natural feminine abilities. As a woman, you have the choice to either embrace and cultivate your natural feminine abilities to bring them in balance with your masculine skills and abilities, or continue to follow the masculine ways of being which have very likely made you successful to date.

As physical embodiments of the feminine, I strongly feel that women have a role to play as lovers, mothers, wives, sisters, and colleagues to be living models of the divine feminine. It is time for women to claim their power with genuine love and compassion toward themselves and for society at large to bring the world into balance. The task at hand is not to overthrow the patriarchal regime in ourselves and society but rather to bring the masculine and feminine principles in balance with each other. In the following chapters we will explore what natural feminine superpowers are, how to cultivate them, and how they could work in harmony with masculine strengths.

CHAPTER 2

Badass at Work Yet Struggle with Love?

The Beauty Contest of Hera, Athena, and Aphrodite

In the Greek myths, Athena, Hera, and Aphrodite enter a contest of beauty and select the young handsome mortal man Paris to judge which of them is the most beautiful. To sway him, each goddess offers him a gift. Hera offers to make him a king of Europe and Asia, Athena offers wisdom and skill in war, and Aphrodite offers him the most beautiful woman in the world. Paris chooses Aphrodite, the goddess of love, to be the most beautiful of them all. This simple man, who really is a metaphor for all men out there, wants love, not power or even wisdom from his companion.

Many of my clients are highly accomplished women in all other areas of their lives, but when it comes to love, they seem to come up against a wall. Living in New York City, I speak to many clients who state that the odds are stacked against them in finding love, but in truth the real reason behind their challenges in love lies in the fact that the very qualities that make them so successful at work are what are causing trouble in their love life.

Here are a few reasons why highly accomplished women have a hard time finding and keeping love.

You Are Used to "Being on Top"

At work, you are never shy about taking charge to get a job done. Unfortunately, a woman who takes charge is often emasculating for men. I am not espousing that women should feign helplessness to be more attractive to men, but quite the opposite. It is not that you are not capable of taking care of yourself; rather, it's more about allowing a man to take care of you to make him feel good, worthy, and strong. Allowing a man to show chivalry with simple acts like opening the door, walking on the side of path closer to traffic, and lending his coat not only makes you feel cared for but lets him feel manly for providing protection and consideration. In love and courtship, there is a constant exchange of bids – bids for affection, bids for worthiness, bids for sex, bids for understanding, bids for forgiveness. A chivalrous gesture by a man is his bid to demonstrate his worthiness. What you may mindlessly do as an act of independence may be in fact rejecting his bid to prove himself worthy, and may eventually drive him away.

Also, there are three stages to all relationships – falling in love, power struggle, and mature love. During the "falling in love" phase, the body is flooded with love hormones to promote physical bonding to ensure continuation of the species. Once the attachment is somewhat established the second phase, the power struggle stage, kicks in. This is where many couples fail to deepen their relationship and give up on the relationship. Women who are used to routinely taking charge like to win and be in the right. Would you rather be right or harmonious? This is often where high-achieving women fail to nurture a relationship. If you were able to embrace your ability to enchant your partner through subtle influence, you would not have to succumb to this typical power struggle phase.

It takes more confidence and inner strength to be yielding than leading.

You Are Independent and Have Yet to Appreciate and Acquire the Virtue of Interdependence

You are likely financially independent and highly self-sufficient, and this enables you more freedom to walk away when things don't go your way. You are used to taking on your share and more, which allows you to be in control of your life. Giving up independence to move toward interdependence is uncomfortable for you because this makes you feel like you are losing control. Layer this with past hurts and defense mechanisms; this makes a perfect cocktail for continued "sovereignty" and control at the price of solitude and loneliness. The truth is that you hide behind independence your fear of becoming vulnerable.

Letting go of control, taking a chance, and becoming vulnerable are exactly what are needed to nurture an intimate relationship.

You Are Goal-Oriented

Being goal-oriented, you are likely to be action and solution oriented. This often leads to living in a state of constant urgency. Your to-do list is always on your mind. You often can't fall asleep because your mind is going a million miles a minute. Healthy relationships require presence, and presence requires a state of being, not doing. Goal-oriented, type-A personality types have a hard time even understanding the concept of being as their lives are full of do, do, do!

Another aspect of the goal-oriented problem solver is that you are probably doing this to your romantic partner, constantly "shoulding" on him by offering him solutions to challenges he may be facing. Yes, the pun is intentional!

Men do not want their partners to solve their problems, if they ever bring them up at all, and this is especially true during the courting phase, where they are trying to prove themselves worthy of your love.

A man wants to appear strong and capable of solving his own problems, especially in the eyes of the woman he loves.

You Are Highly Mental and Analytical

A person with a highly intelligent and analytical mind has most likely overdeveloped their mental capacities. However, femininity and sensuality are embodied. I meet many professional women who are so completely disconnected from their bodies that they are incapable of feeling sensual pleasure. Many women I have met and worked with cannot have an orgasm with their partners. Needless to say, this makes intimacy challenging.

No man wants to feel that they cannot give their lover pleasure. A man's ego would feel more fulfilled being able to truly pleasure his partner than pleasuring himself, which we all know does not take much.

The other downfall of high intelligence is that you mistakenly believe knowing something is sufficient. You can read and understand detailed instructions on how to swim. You can even imagine yourself doing the motions, yet without the direct experience of your body immersed in water, you will never learn how to swim.

Knowing and mentally understanding something and being able to embody and live that knowledge are two completely different things. Knowing that compassion and vulnerability are important for an intimate relationship and then having the courage and resolve to practice are not the same.

One Tibetan lama had told me a story about the relationship between practice and knowledge. In Tibet, they rub butter on leather to keep it soft and supple. The act of rubbing butter is likened to daily practice, while the butter is knowledge. If you leave the butter in the leather satchel for some time, both harden and become completely unusable. Like the butter in the hardened leather satchel, your brain becomes rigid and arrogant. Mistaking knowledge for wisdom gained through practice, you become an intolerable know-it-all.

You Are Highly Disciplined with Rigid Routines

Discipline and routines have allowed you to pack as much as you do in a day. In fact, when you are not able to stick to your routine, like hitting the gym three to five times a week after a forty-plus hour work week, you feel guilty and lazy. But this kind of rigidity does not allow for spontaneity, serendipity, and surprise. How much room can you allow for chance and flow?

Combined with your to-do list and perfectionist standards, there is no room for a relationship. Of course, many will deny this, but I have noticed that many of my clients held the subconscious belief that they didn't have the time or that they couldn't have both success and love. If this is what you believe, this will indeed be your reality.

You Thrive on Challenge and Are Addicted to the Rush

You thrive on and are addicted to winning a challenge and, perhaps unbeknownst to yourself, constantly seek challenges even in relationships. You are attracted to that one brooding unavailable guy despite a bevy of adoring suitors around you. Secretly, you like the challenge to see if you can be the one that changes him. This leads to a string of short- to medium-term relationships that blow up when you finally realize you cannot change him or win him over. You are also often addicted to the drama of the chase, passion, even fights – and the makeup sex, of course!

Now this paints a pretty grim picture of romance for the type-A motivated professional woman, but there is a silver lining. Because you are so motivated to grow and evolve, you do not make excuses or hesitate when you perceive a problem and you respond very quickly to guidance. The only true obstacle for you is becoming aware that your old patterns are not serving you and that you need to find an alternative path and have the humility to reach out for help. It's not your fault that you overdeveloped your masculine qualities because that was precisely what was expected of you. This may have been your past, but it does not have to be your future.

CHAPTER 3

Alpha Bitch to Enchantress

Another week on the road. Anna throws off her heels and collapses on her couch. She is exhausted, but her mind is still racing from the energy of the past week. Some great new wins, and she feels a sense of satisfaction of a job well done. The new CEO certainly noticed the success of the recent board meeting and she is fairly confident she will receive a sizable bonus this year. Dragging her tired body into the shower, she attempts to wash off the stress of the day and eventually settles down in her bed. She pulls out her iPhone to check what her next day entails. Once she is satisfied that she is on top of her schedule, she decides to read a little before going to bed. A few pages in, she hears the familiar "ding" of her phone letting her know that she has a text message.

It's from James. The guy she has been having an on and off relationship with for the past several months. James is handsome and debonair. He claims to "love" her and thinks she is amazing, but the relationship seems to be going nowhere. She wonders if she should respond or ignore it. She really isn't interested in a late-night booty call. She is too exhausted. It's been a while since she last saw him, due to her hectic schedule, and she sometimes wonders if she even has time for a relationship, even though ending up alone is the last thing she wants.

Her ex-boyfriend's words, "You make a great partner, but you are not very sexy," still sting. At work, she has been given the feedback in her last HR assessment that she can be insensitive and too direct.

Femininity, whatever that means, has never been her thing. She was a daddy's girl growing up and she always preferred to climb trees rather than play with dolls. Anna's sister Gina on the other hand was the quintessential girly girl. Unlike Anna, Gina was quiet and obedient. She preferred pretty dresses to Anna's staple uniform of shorts and a t-shirt. Gina's sweet demeanor always got her more positive attention from their parents while Anna was often in hot water due to her rambunctious excursions.

Anna realizes her "masculine" ways have served her well in her career but now starts to wonder what it was costing her. It has been four months since her last menses and her doctor now wants her to go on hormone therapy. She knows her biological clock is ticking and is contemplating freezing her eggs.

As she turns out the lights and lies in bed, she wonders if she is doomed to be an old spinster. She feels a mix of emotions, from sadness and loneliness to numbness about the whole situation. She starts to doze off, thinking, "Maybe you just can't have it all…." Yet, in her wildest fantasies, she dreams of a man who is her equal, who understands her, who desires her passionately and makes her feel like a woman. If she could just meet a guy like that….

Helen was recently promoted to regional Senior Vice President. Part of her is flattered, but on the other hand she feels overwhelmed by her new travel schedule. She is seen as the epitome of class, style, and femininity and is adored by her team. She was the driving force behind the new strategic growth plan presented to the Board and the new investors are eager to meet her.

It has been three years since her divorce and she just heard the news through friends that her ex-husband is expecting a baby with this new wife. When she heard the news, though it pained her, she called to congratulate him. He was a good man, after all. She felt she was to blame for the failure of their marriage. If she had been a bit more available, could things have been different? Then another part of her feels that she never truly loved him. She was more married to her job than her husband. Now that she has just turned forty, Helen wonders if she will ever have children. Though it wasn't ever a priority for her, she always thought she would be a mother one day.

Shortly after separating from her ex-husband, Helen met Patrick. He was intelligent and irresistibly charming. She was swept off her feet and she quickly developed strong feelings and an attachment to him. Unlike her ex-husband, who was stable if a bit boring, Patrick was passionate, emotionally volatile, and unpredictable. But for some crazy reason this made her feel even more attracted to him. She had witnessed him flirting with other women, though he claimed to love her. He made her feel insecure and unsure of herself. Her friends couldn't comprehend what an intelligent, beautiful woman like her was doing losing sleep over and tolerating a guy like Patrick.

Helen wonders herself how she ended up where she is now. Time just seems to have flown by and though now her attachment to Patrick has somewhat cooled, she doesn't feel compelled to officially make a break with him. She is too occupied at work to deal with relationship issues.

Why does Patrick have to make her feel so insecure and unworthy? But more importantly, why can't she just let him go? Clearly, he does not make her feel loved and cherished. While she can be a ball buster with grace at work, why is it that when it comes to men she becomes this indecisive, emotional jumble? Why can't Patrick just make her feel safe and loved?

Do the stories of Anna and Helen ring true to part of your life? Like Anna, do you have trouble with feminine qualities of gentleness and subtlety, or do you relate more to Helen, who has her feminine and masculine aspects in balance at work but when it comes to relationships, loses sight of her personal power?

What if you could be a badass at work – confident, at ease, even graceful, while in your personal relationships you shine from an inner radiance that makes you irresistible and lovable beyond measure? What's more, what if you never had to "chase" or feel rejected by a man again?

It is possible to have it all – love and a career. In fact, when you are fully in your power it is inevitable. This book is about power, specifically feminine power. For too long women have taken on male role models to shape their professional behavior at a great personal cost. In the following chapters we will explore a new definition of femininity for the modern age and how to cultivate it in your daily lives, so you can have the love and life you want.

CHAPTER 4

My Story of Redefining Femininity

I am twenty years old and it is my first day at work. I walk into the company boardroom where all the new hires are supposed to wait for further instructions. I say hi and nod to the three guys already sitting there, waiting with their navy suits, white shirts, and non-descript black shoes. Here I am with my dusty pink suit with plum colored pumps that I thought were oh so chic and professional.

I sit myself down quietly and wait for others to arrive. Three more new hires arrive, all in a navy suit and a white shirt and black shoes. All men. I think to myself, that's okay. They are all guys. Finally, a group of female hires enter, and they are also all wearing navy suits, a white shirt, and non-descript black pumps. Wait! Did I somehow miss a note on company dress code? I stuck out like a sore thumb in the sea of navy suits. Needless to say, it didn't take long for me to fall in line with the others in their navy suits and white shirts and non-descript shoes. But it wasn't just the pastel pink suit that I lost as I joined the navy suit brigade. I also started losing bits of my femininity.

There were very few female role models on Wall Street at the time, and the ones who did make it acted and even looked like men. I was a tomboy and a daddy's girl. I wanted to be like Dad. Being the eager beaver that I was, I started to model and emulate the men around me. After all, this is what I needed to be successful at work, wasn't it?

Fast forward fifteen years. I now work at a multi-billion-dollar hedge fund, where unlike the venerable Wall Street investment banks, the culture is less, let's say, "refined." Though the dress code has relaxed, it is more of a boy's club than ever. I am good at what I do, but I am miserable. Working long hours, even through weekends, as single mom is exhausting. My personal life is a disaster. My five-year-old son hardly sees me.

What kept me sane through those last years in finance was a moving meditation class called *Five Rhythms*. It was essentially an "organic" dance class where I was permitted, and even challenged to, express all the emotions I was holding onto. At first, I was very self-conscious. It was quite a drastic change from my day at work where every word and gesture was calculated. To free myself of my own judgments and ego constraints took a few classes. After a month, I could not live without these classes. On this dance floor I learned how to let the vibrations of music flow through me as if it were a divine voice that let my soul cry out and set me free.

On this dance floor I met my husband. Meeting in this kind of space, where two people can come together in their most honest and true form without the usual social niceties, was refreshing. No lipstick, heels, and hair done to make an impression. Rather, every time we met, my hair was a tangled mess and my makeup smeared or melted away from the sweat. It was a meeting of souls, not our masks that we pretend to be in order to meet societal expectations and conventions.

You may be cringing in your chair, saying to yourself, "I hate to dance. I hate to sing." If so, recognize that this is due to your perfectionist tendencies that would not permit yourself to "be yourself." After all the social conditioning, it is not your fault that you now find your place where freely being and expressing yourself is the last thing you want to do. It is sad but a reality for many of us. We go on pretending all is well, hiding our true radiant and joyful selves behind the veneers of "civilization." If you truly have lost your ability to sing and dance, you are very likely living an empty life.

There is a lot of hype and discussion around diversity and gender inclusion these days. Advocates believe that diversity and gender inclusions will increase profitability and productivity. However, gender or ethnicity alone cannot and will not bring about the desired outcome of diversity. After all, a wolf in lamb's skin is still a wolf. If you hire a bunch of women who are so out of touch with their femininity that they are for all intents and purposes men, how will this create true diversity?

Is it a step in the right direction? Absolutely!

However, it's important to recognize that diversity and inclusion are complex and nuanced, especially in the context of the current male-dominated system of many organizations. What will determine true diversity will be a cultural shift that honors, respects, and embraces different points of view, and, in today's context, values and traits that are traditionally considered feminine. So, then what is femininity and what does it look like at work and life?

What Is Femininity?

The Taoist philosophy of Yin and Yang is perhaps a more accurate understanding of the polarity in nature, often interpreted as feminine and masculine in the Western world. The Taoist definition of these opposing polarities is not limited to or dictated by gender alone.

Whether we call it Yin or Feminine, what kind of traits and values are we talking about?

Fluid vs. Fixed

The feminine is fluid and flexible while the masculine is fixed and constant. Women naturally experience cycles each month and throughout their lifetimes. While men also experience biological cycles, it's not as evident. Also, being more collaborative in nature, women needed to become more adaptable and flexible to accommodate other opinions in the tribe, as well as to adjust to physical changes they experience throughout their lives.

Culturally, girls were praised for being amenable and well-mannered while boys were encouraged to be tough and stalwart. The combination of biology and social indoctrination has led to the fluid and flexible nature of femininity and the fixed and rigid nature of the masculine.

Emotional vs. Logical

The feminine is emotional while the masculine is logical. Renowned neuroscientist Oliver Sacks described a fascinating case of a successful lawyer who had a car accident resulting in severe damage to the amygdala, the emotional center of the brain. After a lengthy recovery period, he seemed to have fully regained his brain functions and returned to work. However, after a few months, a curious development caused him to visit Dr. Sacks. As a lawyer, he could precisely analyze and list pros and cons of any case, yet he could not make a decision as to what course of action to take. Dr. Sacks discovered through this patient that human decision-making is ultimately emotional not logical. Marketers have always known this and thus for decades created ads to appeal to our emotions, not our logical minds.

Masculine society shames emotions as unprofessional, and this is often used as the reason why women are not fit for leadership positions. If Dr. Sacks' assertions are correct, then an individual who is overly logical and lacks emotional competency is less capable of clear and effective decision-making, thus less likely to be a successful leader.

Magnetic vs. Electric

The feminine is magnetic while the masculine is electric. In magnetic force, its very nature is what creates movement (i.e. attract or repel), while an electric force affects change by an active disruption of its object. In other words, magnetic force is created by a state of being, while the electric promotes a state of doing. In Neuro Linguistic Programming practices, the End State Energy, which is an emotional and embodied state of being when one achieves a desired outcome, is utilized to create momentum and clarity in the present moment. Without the right state of being, active doing will result in spinning your wheels with no tangible results.

The feminine at its core is receptive, an inward moving force, the negative polarity, while the masculine is an expanding, an outward moving force, the positive polarity. This is why various spiritual paths compared the feminine to introspective yet ecstatic divine wisdom, and the masculine to skillful means and action.

The natural receptive ability of the feminine, like Mother Earth, has the ability to grow and nurture what is received. I love this quote about the generative nature of women by British novelist and poet William Golding: "*Whatever you give a woman she will make greater. If you give her sperm, she'll give you a baby. If you give her groceries, she'll give you a meal. If you give her a smile, she will give you her heart. She multiplies and enlarges what is given to her.*" Receptivity does not mean passivity. Receiving precedes the generative power of women.

Unfortunately, with the biased view in favor of masculine traits of action and doing, many women lost the ability to receive, which results in more repelling instead of attracting behavior.

Intuitive vs. Empirical

The feminine is intuitive while the masculine is empirical. Intuition comes from a "feeling" or "knowing" that cannot be explained or measured. What cannot be witnessed or measured is dismissed by the masculine as mere superstition, woo-woo nonsense. If you ever have attended a meditation, yoga, or spirituality workshop, you probably noticed that the majority of the attendees are women.

What the masculine often fails to recognize is that tools of measurement evolve, and these means of measurement of even thirty years ago are considered crude by modern standards. The human eyes and ears can only capture a minute portion of the true range of light and sound that surrounds us daily. Scientists have discovered that our conscious mind can process about 8 bits of data per second while our senses are receiving and processing 18 million bits per second. What we think, see, and know is only a tiny fraction of the information available to us.

An insistence on empirical evidence at the expense of intuition can only result in a partial view of the world around us. Intuition comes from the body, a sense of knowing that cannot be rationally explained because our conscious mind just does not have the capacity to do so.

One of the brightest minds of our time, Einstein, once said, "The intuitive mind is a sacred gift and the rational mind is a faithful servant. We have created a society that honors the servant and has forgotten the gift."

Nurturing vs. Inspiring

The feminine is nurturing while the masculine is inspiring. The masculine is able to create momentum, breaking through inertia, and it is the feminine that maintains consistent progress through nurturing. The inspiring leadership style is often seen in pioneers and start-up entrepreneurs as they have the ability to dazzle and inspire those around them to join their cause. However, often these leaders are replaced by a different type of manager once the company is more established and the charismatic start-up leaders are asked to leave.

The feminine nurturing qualities are what sustain life and growth. Though sparks of inspiration are essential to get things started, the steady nurturing force is what is truly needed to ensure that any entity relationship thrives. You see this in romantic relationships: that initial pull and flash of passion draws two people together, however it is the careful nurturing qualities that keep healthy couples together.

Interdependent vs. Specialized

The feminine is interdependent and holistic while the masculine is focused and specialized. Neuroscientists have discovered the different level of development of the white and grey matter in the brain indeed supports this statement. The grey matter, which is the data processing centers, is activated ten times more in men. While white matter, which is the networking channels that connect the grey matter, is activated seven times more in women. This translates to focus and tunnel vision in men while women are able to take a more holistic view of the situation.

In hunter-gatherer societies, this allowed men to be able to focus on prey and successfully provide for the tribe. With the overdeveloped white matter in women, women had a more developed peripheral vision and proprioception, enabling them to keep an eye on the children while tending the fire and preparing a meal.

As civilization started to move away from these tribal societies to massive urban centers, men started to dominate and control the various social organizations. One area where this shows up clearly is medicine. Hippocrates, father of modern medicine, believed in the holistic treatment of the body. His first course of treatment was a change in diet. In modern times, with the specialization of different fields within medicine, holistic approaches are considered "alternative," not the primary course of action. This resulted in a sharp rise in chronic ailments that do not respond well to modern medicine.

Being the mother of two boys, growing up with no male siblings or cousins around, I perused a number of parenting books for boys. My main take away was the importance of the "pack" and their pecking order within it. A masculine society is competitive by nature and Mother Nature designed it precisely that way to ensure the successful evolution of the species. The strongest, healthiest, and most desirable were able to mate and produce progeny. It is no wonder that there is so much ego and puffing up of the chest in the masculine world.

On the other hand, the feminine depended upon collaboration to survive in tribal society. To be likeable and procure favors was the main currency among women. While the unbalanced masculine results in an over-inflated ego and a tyrannical nature, the unbalanced feminine gives way to self-doubt, lack of independent thought, and an overly-giving nature, essentially a doormat.

Natural vs. Civilized

The feminine is natural and wild while the masculine is industrial and civilized. In many ancient indigenous spiritual traditions life, nature, seasons, and time were represented in a sacred wheel. The North represented winter and father while the South was the domain of summer and mother. In these cultures, the North and masculine were the aspects of industry, mental power, and determination, while the South and feminine were the aspects of the wild unknown.

This is reminiscent of Freud's theory of the Ego vs. Id. The North represents Ego, the conscious mind, and civilization, while the South, the Id, is the subconscious mind, which is that enigmatic part of you that is truly shaping your emotions, behavior, and life. The ability to embrace, harness, direct, and channel the inherent power in the wild unknown feminine is essential to your path to stepping in to your personal power.

Embodied vs. Mental

The feminine is embodied while the masculine is conceptual. According to Kabbalists, the universe is made up of the emanation of levels of energy from the Creator. This is expressed in what the Kabbalists call the Tree of Life. *Keter*, which is the first form of emanation and considered masculine, is unmanifested pure potentiality, in human terms, a mental construct. This physical dimension we live in is called *Malchut* and is considered feminine and the final form of emanation. Many spiritual traditions and world cultures call the sky Father Sky, and earth, Mother Earth. There seems to be universal consensus dating back to tribal times of physicality or embodiment as feminine.

The body is what enables us to feel sensation and have emotions. Historically, in many spiritual and secular societies, the body was maligned to be sinful, the cause of suffering and temptation, and the base animal side of humanity. As a result, these societies created cultures that punished and demeaned sensuality. But this is not ancient history. I have met several clients that unconsciously believed that their bodies were sinful and not to be trusted or that the body was messy and dirty. Not surprisingly, these highly mental women were never able to experience orgasm with a partner.

Scientists now know that memory is not simply stored in the brain. Memory is stored in every single cell of your body. The body holds an immense amount of wisdom and information that is untapped by most.

I discussed at length the contrasting feminine and masculine qualities in all of us. In this exploration, I do not want to give an impression that the feminine is superior to the masculine in any way. The reason for this investigation is to create a balance between the two. For many millennia, feminine qualities were either maligned, ignored, or unappreciated, and thus highlighting the need and power of these attributes seemed necessary.

The FEMININE Path

In today's modern society, the masculine mode has guided and defined leadership, standards of achievement, education, medicine, and even attitudes toward romance and sex. The lack of appreciation for feminine qualities has led to a society where stress is the norm to a point where over 70% of people over fifty are on long-term medication; domestic violence is common place; the environment is toxic; the number of children with autism and ADHD is rising; and 80% of women have body image insecurities due to media distortion of the female form.[5] As the various age-old prophecies state, it is time for the "soft light of the moon" to rise. And as the embodiment of the feminine, women have a responsibility to create this shift.

So now that we have a broader, if not better, understanding of femininity and what is at stake, what are the next steps toward embracing and cultivating these qualities?

In this book, we will further explore each of the above-mentioned feminine attributes and how they become a source of power in our lives. Here is a quick preview of the feminine superpowers to be explored in the coming chapters.

- **F**luidity and flexibility are the source of adaptability and malleability in our characters that creates *true resilience and subtle yet powerful influence*

- **E**motions are energy in motion. They are the source of our *passion and drive* to evolve and grow

- **M**agnetism and Mystery are the secret to the Law of Attraction and *working in the invisible quantum domain*

- **I**ntuition is the power of *inner knowing beyond logic* and limited human consciousness

- **N**urturance is the *expansive and transformative power of compassion* and empathy

- **I**nterdependence is the mode that allows for *higher perception and wisdom*

- **N**ature holds the secret to *healing and physical, emotional, and mental health*
- **E**mbodiment offers an opening to the power of *presence and enlightenment*

CHAPTER 5

Femininity Quotient Assessment

Now that we have a map of the path forward, it is time to figure out where you are. Even the most accurate of maps is useless if you are unclear on where you stand. Answer the questions below, adding up the total for each section, and then add up the grand total in the table below. See where your feminine strengths are and where there is some room for improvement. If there is a specific area you find particularly weak, you may want to pay close attention while reading that chapter.

Fluidity

___ I don't mind unexpected changes.

(Yes = 1, No = 0)

___ Change excites and motivates me.

(Yes = 1, No = 0)

___ In conflict, I first explore more subtle and diplomatic ways of expressing myself.

(Yes = 1, No = 0)

___ I am not easily ruffled when things don't go my way. I can quickly bounce back.

(Yes = 1, No = 0)

___ When someone is angry or upset with me I let it roll off my back.

(Yes = 1, No = 0)

___ I like learning about new things and different ways to do things.

(Yes = 1, No = 0)

___ I like doing things spontaneously without a fixed plan.

(Yes = 1, No = 0)

___ I generally don't have strong opinions about things and can see other points of view.

(Yes = 1, No = 0)

___ My body is flexible and supple.

(Yes = 1, No = 0)

___ I am open-minded.

(Yes = 1, No = 0)

F TOTAL: _____

Emotions

___When I am angry I hold it back.

(Yes = 0, No = 1)

___I am in touch with my feelings.

(Yes = 1, No = 0)

___ I know how to process my emotions without stuffing it or vomiting them on others.

(Yes = 1, No = 0)

___ When I get emotional I behave irrationally in a way that I regret later.

(Yes = 0, No = 1)

___ I know how to channel my emotions in a healthy way.

(Yes = 1, No = 0)

___ When I get upset, I stay that way for a long time.

(Yes = 0, No = 1)

____ I know how to express emotions in a healthy way.

(Yes = 1, No = 0)

____ I am aware of how different emotions feel in my body.

(Yes = 1, No = 0)

____ I am not afraid to feel my emotions.

(Yes = 1, No = 0)

____ I am not afraid or hesitant to express my emotions.

(Yes = 1, No = 0)

E TOTAL: _____

Magnetism

____ I understand the concept of divine timing.

(Yes = 1, No = 0)

____ I know how to attract attention without being overt about it.

(Yes = 1, No = 0)

____ I am patient.

(Yes = 1, No = 0)

____ I know when to act and when to hold back.

(Yes = 1, No = 0)

____ My primary mode is to act first.

(Yes = 0, No = 1)

____ I understand that there is divine timing to important events.

(Yes = 1, No = 0)

____ I know how to relax when my job is done.

(Yes = 1, No = 0)

____ I trust the Universe.

(Yes = 1, No = 0)

____ I understand that there are more things at play than my actions.

(Yes = 1, No = 0)

____ I know that I attract more of what I feel.

(Yes = 1, No = 0)

M TOTAL: _____

Intuition

____ I often get prophetic dreams.

(Yes = 1, No = 0)

____ I know when someone is thinking of me.

(Yes = 1, No = 0)

___ I often notice synchronicities.

(Yes = 1, No = 0)

___ I have often known the outcome of situations before they happen. (Yes = 1, No = 0)

___ I get a "gut" feeling about things.

(Yes = 1, No = 0)

___ I trust my intuition and act on it.

(Yes = 1, No = 0)

___ I get confused about the messages from my intuition.

(Yes = 0, No = 1)

___ I know when someone is lying.

(Yes = 1, No = 0)

___ My intuition is spot on.

(Yes = 1, No = 0)

___ I am a good judge of character both at work and in romance.

(Yes = 1, No = 0)

I TOTAL: _____

Nurturance

___ I am a good listener.

(Yes = 1, No = 0)

___ People often come to me for advice, especially around personal matters.

(Yes = 1, No = 0)

___ People trust me.

(Yes = 1, No = 0)

___ I like helping others.

(Yes = 1, No = 0)

___ I know how to calm someone when they are upset.

(Yes = 1, No = 0)

___ I know how to encourage someone when they are down and depressed.

(Yes = 1, No = 0)

___ I have a calming effect on people.

(Yes = 1, No = 0)

___ I can sense other people's pain viscerally.

(Yes = 1, No = 0)

___ I am good with self-care.

(Yes = 1, No = 0)

___ I know how to nourish myself.

(Yes = 1, No = 0)

N TOTAL: _____

Interdependence

___ I am comfortable asking for help when I need it.

(Yes = 1, No = 0)

___ I am comfortable receiving compliments.

(Yes = 1, No = 0)

___ In conflict, I say what is with compassion.

(Yes = 1, No = 0)

___ I am able to see both sides of a story.

(Yes = 1, No = 0)

___ I look for ways to collaborate.

(Yes = 1, No = 0)

___ I prefer to collaborate over competing.

(Yes = 1, No = 0)

___ I am good at finding win-win situations.

(Yes = 1, No = 0)

___ I am comfortable being vulnerable.

(Yes = 1, No = 0)

____ I have healthy boundaries.

(Yes = 1, No = 0)

____ I know when and how to give and when to receive.

(Yes = 1, No = 0)

I TOTAL: _____

Nature

____ I have no problems falling asleep and sleeping soundly.

(Yes = 1, No = 0)

____ I know when my body needs rest and make sure to listen to my body's needs.

(Yes = 1, No = 0)

____ I feel happy and refreshed in the great outdoors.

(Yes = 1, No = 0)

____ I am good with plants.

(Yes = 1, No = 0)

____ I understand and feel the healing properties of nature.

(Yes = 1, No = 0)

____ Nature touches me.

(Yes = 1, No = 0)

____ I prefer the comforts of civilization to the outdoors.

   (Yes = 0, No = 1)

____ I am comfortable being myself in any situation.

   (Yes = 1, No = 0)

____ I feel free and natural in my body.

   (Yes = 1, No = 0)

____ Nature nourishes me.

   (Yes = 1, No = 0)

N TOTAL: _____

Embodiment

____ I have a sense of my energetic body.

   (Yes = 1, No = 0)

____ I seek and appreciate sensual pleasures including sex.

   (Yes = 1, No = 0)

____ If I close my eyes and scan my body I can feel and connect to every part of my body.

   (Yes = 1, No = 0)

____ I am easily bored so I constantly look for something to do.

   (Yes = 0, No = 1)

____ I have a healthy body image.

(Yes = 1, No = 0)

____ I eat healthy and stay active.

(Yes = 1, No = 0)

____ I embrace my sensuality.

(Yes = 1, No = 0)

____ I love and appreciate my body.

(Yes = 1, No = 0)

____ I am aware of the signals my body sends me.

(Yes = 1, No = 0)

____ I love to dance and express myself in a physical way.

(Yes = 1, No = 0)

____ I know that my body is a temple and treat it that way.

(Yes = 1, No = 0)

E TOTAL: _____

F	E	M	I	N	I	N	E	TOTAL

Assessment Key

If you scored below a six in any one category you may want to focus on those areas of growth. However, being of different constitutions and temperaments, there are certain feminine attributes that come naturally to some while others are more challenging. The total scores show your overall Femininity Quotient.

Up to 25: Femininity Isn't Your Cup of Tea

It is very likely that you actively reject the feminine in favor of masculine qualities. You feel that femininity is weak, overly emotional, and wishy-washy. You prefer logic to intuition and prefer to have a plan ahead of time. Uncertainty makes you feel uncomfortable. It is very likely that you have trouble in relationships, and if you are in a relationship your partner probably takes on more feminine qualities. If this works for you, great! But if you are not happy with where things are, make sure to take your time with each chapter and do the exercises with an open mind.

26 – 60: Room for Improvement

It is likely that there are some areas in which you excel and others in which you certainly need some help. Focus on the chapters in the areas you scored lowest in. Make sure to explore areas in your life where these areas of improvement are showing up.

61+: You are in Feminine Flow, a Goddess Incarnate.

You embrace the Goddess within, but there are always higher levels you can reach. Continue to deepen your understanding of the divine feminine within you. Actively cultivate a relationship with you inner Goddess by the use of an altar as discussed in Chapter 10 and a daily ritual to strengthen the divine feminine within.

CHAPTER 6

Power of Fluidity

Nothing is softer or more flexible than water,
yet nothing can resist it.

– Lao-Tzu

Water is one of the most important natural elements of life. The average adult human body is 50–65% water. The percentage of water in infants is much higher, typically around 75–78% water, dropping to 65% by one year of age. Body composition varies according to gender and fitness level because fatty tissue contains less water than lean tissue. The level of water in our body is indicative of the level of life force in our body, as evidenced by the higher level of water in infants and lean tissue. Water is a primary source of life and the fountain of youth.

Lama Tsultrim says in her book *Wisdom Rising*:

Water is a fascinating element because it appears in so many forms. It can be steam, liquid, ice, froth, wavy, flowing, or still. Water can be gentle but destructive. It is a very powerful element. Even when water appears gentle, it has a penetrating ability, [which can] gently eat away something as hard as stone.

In this chapter we will explore the feminine power of fluidity. While the masculine draws strength from its fixed and constant qualities, the feminine power comes from its ever-changing aspect. During a mighty storm, the tall, rigid oak will break but the seemingly insignificant blades of grass and the tall bamboo sway with the wind, emerging unaffected.

The Willow Tree

During one of my meditations, I was shown the willow tree as a metaphor for the feminine power of fluidity. Visiting my muses and metaphysical guides, they led me to a beautiful spot underneath a willow tree. The ground was covered with soft moss and above me were the sweeping swaying branches of the willow tree. When asked to show me the way of feminine power, my guide simply looked up and gently touched the swinging branches of the willow tree.

For the Celts, the willow tree is the goddess tree and was known for its close connection with water and the moon. Willow tree branches were used in ceremonies for enhancement of intuitive abilities to produce a clearer understanding of the world.

The willow tree's most treasured trait is its suppleness. The willow tree is one of the few trees that can bend to extreme shapes without breaking. The willow is a fertile grower and has the ability to take root from a single branch that falls in a marshy bog. This ability to survive and thrive in marshy bogs is the reason why the willow tree is planted, to stabilize and drain soft, boggy, unusable land.

The message of the willow trees is to adjust to life's challenges with fluidity rather than fight them with a fixed mindset. Not only is the willow able to survive, it has the power to thrive in the most challenging conditions and even transform them.

The Monkeys of Koshima Island

There was a group of monkeys in Japan that had been observed in the wild for a period of over thirty years. In 1952, on the island of Koshima, scientists gave monkeys sweet potatoes dropped in sand. The monkeys liked the taste of the raw sweet potatoes, but they didn't like the dirt.

An eighteen-month-old female accidentally dropped her sweet potato in a stream and found she liked it much better. She then started washing the sweet potatoes before she ate them and taught this trick to her mother. Her playmates also learned this new way and they taught their mothers, too. This cultural innovation (by monkey standards) was gradually picked up by various monkeys. In six years all the young monkeys learned to wash the sandy sweet potatoes.

So, the order of change happened from a young female monkey who influenced her mother, other young females and males followed, and it wasn't until a tipping point was reached that the older male monkeys followed suit.

Now, you may think this is just a story of monkeys, but look at new fashion trends. Designers are constantly looking for what hip females are doing, as they are usually the forefront of any new trend. The feminine is more adaptable to change and with the current pace of change in technology and society this quality of flexibility and adaptability will be critical in our personal and professional lives.

Attachment, the Bane of Fluidity

What keeps us stuck and rigid is attachment. This can be to a lover, child, friend, job, location, and sometimes even your own identity. One thing that is guaranteed to never change is change itself. When you are fixed on a specific condition you inevitably invite disappointment and grief into your life.

Nadine was a successful senior executive in a large NY hedge fund. At work, she was the iron lady, always steady and unshakeable. Yet behind the flawless façade was a lonely and shut down woman. She had been married and divorced once and since then, with no children in the picture, put all her energy into work.

As younger and hungry junior partners moved up the ranks wanting to shift the strategic direction of the firm, she felt annoyed and even resentful at these upstarts. Nadine's routines were fixed and predictable. She did not like surprises and every hour of her day was spoken for.

However, one day everything shifted. The new head of her department was one of those young upstarts. She started to get marginalized at work and was not given recognition for deals that she helped win and close. The signs were clear that she needed to move on, yet she was not able or even willing to see beyond her current role and routine. Eventually, she was asked to leave with a handsome "severance" check. Despite the fact that she was financially set for life, she found no joy in this newfound freedom and possibility. In fact, she was not even able to see her new situation in that light.

She felt disgraced and regretful. Without her job, she did not know what do with herself. She was attached to her firm, her routines, and most significantly, her social status and identity as a partner in her firm. When this was taken away from her, she sank into a depression. In her mind, she had sacrificed everything for her career and now she had nothing to show for it.

For Nadine it was her job and the status that came along with it, but I have also seen similar struggles in women who have become empty nesters as single mothers. Your energy and attention were fixed on serving and caring for others and now that "responsibility" is taken away, you feel lost and rudderless. Now you are forced to look inwards and explore what your deepest and truest dreams may be. The structures that molded you to be a certain way are gone and now you are the one that must redefine who you are.

The Paradox of Control

The need to control creates rigidity and a fixed mindset and attachment to a specific outcome that more often than not leads to disappointment, yet it is probably one of the most common traits I see in high-powered women. Natural attention to detail also comes with the need to fix what is out of place. Year after year, positive feedback from this kind of behavior in the form of career success slowly hardens the mind against the unknown to the point of fear. Everything must be just so. Everything must be in place.

The paradox of control is that the more you try to control a situation, the more you are truly giving up your personal power and causing a drain of energy. This may not be as apparent when everything is going your way, but the moment an unexpected change happens, the survival mode instincts kick in and you end up in a whirlwind of emotions, taking away your ability to make sensible decisions. An apt metaphor would be crossing a river. You need to get from point A, where you are, to point B, across the river. The shortest distance between points A and B is a straight line, so you decide that will be your path. If the flow of the river is slow and gentle and offers very little resistance, you would be able to stay on the path with relative ease. However, if the water is flowing fast with many obstacles along the way, staying on the straight line would not only be challenging, it could be perilous. The lesson of this metaphor may seem obvious to you, but I see so many women struggle to fight and control things that are simply not in their control. Where could you be doing this in your life?

Gina is a brilliant, driven, and successful executive in her later thirties. It has been three years since her last serious relationship. A few months into our work together, she finally met someone she felt attracted to and quickly became "obsessed." He fit the bill. Unfortunately, after a few months, his interest seemed to wane, and he started not responding to her emails or texts. She was baffled. She thought all was well. She felt rejected and humiliated and this led her to overanalyze every aspect of their short-lived relationship. She could not control what was going on and she could not accept what was happening either.

This single-mindedness had served her well at work, giving her the ability to control and anticipate all challenges and overcome them. Yet in relationships, this made her come across as grasping and controlling.

I offered Gina the *Contemplation of Birds in Sight*. Every person that comes into your life is like a bird that flies into your field of sight. You have no control over whether that particular bird will stay for a brief moment or build a nest and stick around. Any sense of control you think you may have is an illusion. You can make your environment more attractive, yet ultimately whether they decide to leave, or stay is out of your control. The moment you try to control the situation, the situation is now controlling you. Gina lost sight of her true desire, which was to have a loving and committed relationship, but instead she got fixated on a person and lost sight of her true destination. We worked together to implement a strong daily practice that allowed her to stay grounded and open.

Gina understood that her controlling ways were hurting her and with this realization, she made a conscious shift. There was a softening in her that was evident in her face and composure. Shortly after, there were some drastic strategic and personnel changes in her company that jeopardized her career. Normally, this type of unexpected change would send her into a tizzy that would keep her up at night and leave her anxious and tense. Instead, she was completely unfazed. In fact, she seemed positively relaxed and calm. She accepted the situation as it was and plotted her best course of action based on what was presented to her.

Fluidity in the Face of Confrontation or Adversity

Nadine wondered if things could have turned out differently for her. In hindsight, she realized her obstinate attitude toward new shifts in the firm was what made her fall out of favor with management. Her negotiation style at work and in relationships had always been cool and immovable.

Nadine met her ex-husband, Paul, at work. They were both starting their careers in finance as analysts straight out of college. They seemed to be a perfect match on paper. They both went to a prestigious university and graduated with honors. They were a handsome and ambitious couple and already had many friends in common.

After a couple of years of dating, they got married. However, things got rocky right away. They were both focused on their careers and were both traveling a lot. Paul wanted to start a family, but Nadine preferred to wait a few more years. This conflict created an invisible wall between them. Eventually Paul had an affair and left Nadine.

Fluidity allows you to see situations from different perspectives and allows for you to be more agreeable in nature. It also allows you to influence others by giving them space to come to their own conclusions.

When it comes to relating with men, boys are encouraged to be stalwart and determined. The male brain is also wired to be more narrowly focused or have tunnel vision. When in disagreement, the feminine power lies in its ability to be "gentle and penetrating" like water. Of course, there are situations in which a show of strength is warranted, like a tsunami razing a village to the ground. Yet, I find that situations that require this kind of drastic approach in daily life are rare. Then, what does this look like?

Gandhi, Jesus, Martin Luther King, and Mother Theresa are some world leaders that understood the power drawn from gentle yet penetrating approach of water. It takes much more inner strength and deep wisdom to take a gentle peaceful stance than to respond with brute force or anger in the face of adversity.

Cultivating the Power of Fluidity

So then, how do you remain gentle and penetrating in conflict? Also, how do you develop discernment to know when you need to take the tsunami approach? Mindful fluidity is powerful. Being a pushover or doormat because you have poor boundaries and low self-esteem should not be mistaken for being fluid or flexible.

The power of fluidity comes from a deep trust in yourself and your values that gives rise to the ability to not be attached to any one outcome. This kind of wisdom allows you to have a broader perspective, enabling you to see other points of views, as well as have the humility to know that there may be yet another outcome that you just don't see at the moment. When you are attached you become fixed and inflexible. Your vision narrows, and you end up losing the forest for the trees. There are three keys to fluidity:

Stay Curious

An important key to cultivating fluidity is to be curious. Curiosity keeps you open and nimble. Nadine, whom I spoke of earlier, stopped being curious. She was a recognized expert in her field and this lulled her into a false sense of omniscience and the feeling that she no longer needed to grow and evolve. This became her downfall. Instead of being curious about her ex-husband's motivations to have a family or the new strategic direction of her firm, she felt that she knew what was best. Truth be told, the inability to be curious really comes from an insecurity and fear of the unknown. Fear makes us rigid and contracted, hence the expression "frozen in fear." Curiosity keeps us alert to our changing circumstances, which in turn enables us to respond proactively to unanticipated situations.

Let Go of Attachments

There is a Zen story about a poor farmer who had a son. One day a beautiful wild stallion came to graze in their fields and did not leave. The neighbors said, "How lucky you are to have acquired such a beautiful horse by chance." The farmer simple replied, "Maybe so, maybe not." After a few months, the stallion escaped the stables and disappeared. The neighbors then said how unlucky he was to lose the stallion. Again, the farmer replied, "Maybe so, maybe not." A week later, the stallion returned, this time with a whole herd of horses. The neighbors were surprised and again expressed how lucky he was. The farmer replied the same: "Maybe so, maybe not." One day, his son was trying to tame one of these horses and fell off and broke his leg, leaving him with a permanent limp. The neighbors commented on how unlucky he was that his only son was now lame, at which the farmer simply replied, "Maybe so, maybe not." Shortly thereafter a war broke out in the country and all the young men were conscripted to the army. The lame son, of course, was not taken because of his limp. The moral of the story is that we often judge what is good or not based on a narrow short-term view. An injury or challenge can be a blessing in disguise. Choose to have the humility to recognize that your vision is quite limited, so you can let go of any attachments to any desired outcome. This does not mean that you don't have goals or direction. It simply means that you are able to adapt to new situations without wasting energy on resisting what is.

Keep Your Eyes on the True Prize

Would you rather be right or happy? Keeping your eye on the true prize allows you to be fluid under adverse circumstances. When you get into a spat with your significant other or colleague, you could either choose to dig in your heels and try to persuade them of your views or you could choose to be gentle and penetrating. You are able to achieve this when you remember to keep your eye on the prize, which is to have a harmonious and respectful relationship with them. Most arguments, no matter how significant they seem at the time, are really frivolous and silly when you are able to look back at them from a calmer state. Whatever conflict or challenge you are facing, how much will being right about it matter on your deathbed? If the answer is "It doesn't matter," then yield like a willow branch, but if the answer is that it will matter to you on your deathbed, then that is the time for the tsunami approach.

Fluidity allows you to thrive in seemingly adverse situations. It gives you the ability to be resilient, creative, and adaptable. For Nadine, losing her job was the wakeup call to recognize the importance of fluidity. When you are rigid and fixed, life often throws you dramatic circumstances to jolt you out of your stagnant and static state. The fundamental nature of life is change and resisting this is an exhausting and ultimately futile endeavor. Einstein said, *"The measure of intelligence is the ability to change."*

☙

EXERCISE: Cultivate the Power of Fluidity through Shapeshifting

Being able to adapt yourself to different circumstances is at the core of the power of fluidity. In many indigenous practices around the world, there are stories of shapeshifting. I was skeptical of this until during an ecstatic dance session, I spontaneously fell into a trance and felt myself transform into a black jaguar.

Though my human mind was aware of what was happening, my instincts, desires, and behavior shifted to that of a wild jungle cat. I started hissing and clawing at things like a jaguar would. Then I noticed another jaguar in the midst. There was another dancer who had shapeshifted into a jaguar. All I could think of was this other was in *my* territory. We hissed and clawed at each other, circling each other. A battle of sorts took place and I won. I claimed the territory and the other cat slunk away. I felt triumphant, like a jaguar would feel fending off a trespasser. I felt no self-consciousness about my behavior because during this event

I was no longer human. I eventually came back into my own "skin" but the power of the transformation stayed with me. Since this experience, I have been able to merge, converse, and learn from non-human beings such as trees, crystals, and natural elements.

Shapeshifting is about shifting your energy. Here is an excerpt from a conversation John Perkins has with a Mayan elder shaman from his book *Shapeshifting*:

"Spirit is energy."

"It is?"

"Energy is everything."

"So, when people say they see spirits, it is the energy they see."

"Yes"

"You have to accept that you already are the same as the thing you're going to shift into – that your separateness is only an illusion. You also must believe that there is no hierarchy, that you as human being are no higher on some evolutionary chart than you as tree or jaguar."

The value of shapeshifting is that when we are able to make this energetic shift, we are imbued with the power and essence of the form we shapeshift into.

There might be moments where this may feel silly and superstitious or you may have an intense experience that makes you feel like you are going crazy. I have been through both sentiments in my journey. My advice is instead of judging and trying to understand what is going on, have fun with it like a curious child. Children are constantly "modeling" the adults around them. Shapeshifting at its essence is modeling so that you take on new helpful qualities and abilities.

For this exercise, we will transform into all forms and temperaments of water.

1. Download the Spotify App on your computer or mobile device.

2. Search for **Shapeshifting to Water** playlist.

3. Follow the playlist.

4. Once the playlist is cued, make sure you have a large enough space to move around freely.

5. As you listen to playlist, let the vibration of the music imbue each of your cells.

6. Let your body move to the vibration you feel.

7. Do not think but rather move spontaneously as your body wishes to move. Dance, move, and vibrate to the music. Einstein said dancers are the athletes of God. Let the divine stir in you without judgment.

8. Journal upon completing to record what insights arose during your shapeshift.

CHAPTER 7

Power of Emotions

Diana was finally able to let go of her past relationship and start dating again. At first, she became excited by the number of dates she was able to schedule using dating applications, but this excitement quickly turned to disillusionment in a few short weeks when the dates did not amount to anything meaningful. The ones she was attracted to seemed aloof and unavailable while the ones she did not feel any "chemistry" with would pursue her with ardor.

In these short few weeks, she went through a roller coaster of emotions. She started to wonder, *What is wrong with me? Why am I always attracted to the guys who aren't into me?* What she did not realize was that she was re-enacting emotional patterns that she learned as a child around love and affection.

Emotions and Energy

Emotion is energy in motion. On a biological level, energy in the form of ATP produced by our mDNA is what gives us life. Energy is used to fuel everything our body does. Even our thoughts and emotions require and are an expression of energy. The Taoist called this life force energy *qi* or *chi;* the Vedics called it *prana* and Polynesian cultures called it *mana*. It was also known as *pnuema* in ancient Greece, *manitou* by the Native Americans, *ruah* in Judaism.

Dr. Joe Dispenza states in his book *Becoming Supernatural*:

When we think a thought, those networks of neurons that fire in our brain create electrical charges. When those thoughts also cause a chemical reaction that results in a feeling or an emotion, those feelings create magnetic charges. They merge with the thoughts that create the electric charges to produce a specific electromagnetic field equal to your state of being.

In other words, your thoughts charged with emotion create your state of being and, further, an electromagnetic field around you. Some call this your aura. This energy field has the power to influence those around you. You have felt it when someone angry walks in the room or when you are around someone who is deeply grieving. They may be trying to hide it but your "sixth sense" will likely feel the electromagnetic field that they created through their emotions.

Your emotions determine your behavior and life view, which ultimately shapes your future. You can choose to stay enslaved by your emotion's being and at the whim of whatever life throws at you, or you can actively shift your *state of being* to change your life.

This requires carefully tracking and reviewing your emotions. However, this can be challenging as it is very likely that you are so used to *being* a certain way that you may not be aware of what thoughts and emotions pervade your state of being. According to researchers, we have 50,000 to 70,000 thoughts a day, or 35 to 48 thoughts per minute. With the constant stream of thoughts, it is not realistic to track them effectively. However, observing your emotions is something that is easily achievable, as our emotions create a stronger imprint on our memory. Yet, your emotions are often inscrutable while you are in the thick of it, so it helps to have a detailed map of your emotional landscape.

Map of Consciousness

Dr. Hawkins in his book *Power vs. Force: The Hidden Determinants of Human Behavior* laid out an insightful map of human emotions, motivations, and its internal processes.

Using kinesiology, he was able to create a scale of levels of human consciousness.

	Scale	Emotion	Level	Internal Process	Life View
S **T** **R** **O** **N** **G**	700-1000	Ineffable	Enlightenment	Pure Consciousness	Is
	600	Bliss	Peace	Illumination	Perfect
	540	Serenity	Joy	Transfiguration	Complete
	500	Reverence	Love	Revelation	Benign
	400	Understanding	Reason	Abstraction	Meaningful
	350	Forgiveness	Acceptance	Transcendence	Merciful
	310	Optimism	Willingness	Intention	Inspiring
	250	Trust	Neutrality	Release	Enabling
	200	Affirmation	Courage	Empowerment	Permitting
W **E** **A** **K**	175	Scorn	Pride	Inflation	Indifferent
	150	Hate	Anger	Aggression	Vengeful
	125	Craving	Desire	Enslavement	Denying
	100	Anxiety	Fear	Withdrawal	Punitive
	75	Regret	Grief	Despondency	Disdainful
	50	Despair	Apathy	Abdication	Condemning
	30	Blame	Guilt	Destruction	Vindictive
	20	Humiliation	Shame	Elimination	Despising

Figure 1: Map of Consciousness sourced from Power vs. Force by David Hawkins

At the bottom of the scale is humiliation, which is caused by the consciousness level of shame. Let's say you were rejected by your lover and feel humiliated. Your level of consciousness is at that moment shame of not being good enough. Your thoughts are likely to be that you were not smart enough, pretty enough, slim enough, or perhaps kind enough. Your thoughts come from a deep shame of lack.

If you then shift from shame to, let's say, desire to be with your lover, you are now enslaved and become needy and perhaps obsessive about the object of your love, exhibiting behaviors like waiting by the phone and hanging onto his every word. Alternatively, perhaps you are in a long-term relationship and from feeling the shame of rejection, to protect yourself you shift toward apathy. You may feel trapped and in despair with a lack of hope. Whether it is shame, desire, or apathy, when these levels of consciousness become your patterned internal process your life views emerge.

According to Dr. Hawkins, those who have been subject to repeated humiliation and shamed as a tool of parenting and punishment often compensate with perfectionism, becoming rigid, overly driven, judgmental, and intolerant. My client Diana was raised by a strict and religious mother who often compared her to others and shamed her if she did not perform up to the high standards she set for her daughter. This kind of exacting scrutiny is how Diana's mother expressed love. Anna had to perform and be perfect to be lovable. Just as Dr. Hawkins described, Diana grew up to be a perfectionist, ambitious, highly intelligent, and accomplished, yet rigid, critical, and markedly unfeminine.

When her ambitious nature took over her feeling of lack, Diana would become obsessed with her object of affection. She would spend hours overanalyzing every interaction and poring over her lover's social profiles over and over again. Then she would become ashamed of her behavior and drop to a feeling of humiliation and not being good enough again. In this vicious cycle between shame and desire, she was trapped and unable to see the beautiful, intelligent, and powerful woman that she is.

Transmuting the Energy of Emotions

Counter-intuitive as it may seem, when Diana was trapped in this cycle I guided her toward feeling anger. Instead of going from shame to desire, I asked her to find reasons to become angry at her lover's inconsiderate behavior. She resisted at first. In fact, it almost seemed like she did not know how to be angry for herself. I explained to her that anger was the first step toward elevating her level of consciousness and taking back the power she gave to her lover over her self-worth.

Anger has immense energy behind it and can be used to catapult into freedom from old patterns. Once Diana was able to feel anger, with a little guidance she was quickly able to create emotional boundaries for herself and then pride in who she was and all that she had to offer. From there, without any prompting, she started feeling understanding and even gratitude toward her inconsiderate lover for the opportunity to learn about emotional boundaries and self-empowerment.

Little girls are encouraged to be agreeable and congenial. Many spiritual paths talk about the danger and damage anger can cause but do not teach how to process or use it. During my own journey, I proactively moved away from feeling so-called "negative" emotions because it was not "spiritual." This all changed when I met a kind Korean Tao Master, Sarah Choi, who told me that I diminished my personal power by stuffing or denying my emotions. Emotions are different states of energy and by denying them, I was cutting myself at the foot. All emotions have power that can be harnessed and directed toward personal growth.

Every emotion has a purpose. Anger can be directed to action and breaking free from old patterns. Grief, unlike anger, is a sinking and cooling feeling. If you can become aware and accept grief, you can see it for it is – a state of energy. While anger propels action, grief can cultivate introspection and contemplation. The energy of grief is directed inward and can be used to achieve a sense of grounding and even a state of non-attachment. Instead of blindly reacting to emotions, recognize that your emotions do not define you and that they are a transient stage of energy that will eventually pass. So, take advantage of the emotions when they arise.

I find having the Map of Consciousness printed and posted somewhere visible is helpful until this chart becomes completely internalized. It is a nice reference to help you track where you are in your level of consciousness. You can download a PDF copy on my website at www.sukisohn.com/resources

Your Natural Elements

You are born with natural preferences as defined by your genetic code. Ancient healers across the world used the metaphor of natural elements to understand human physical constitution, behavioral traits, and emotional landscapes. Different parts of the world used varying combinations and numbers of elements, but the common core are fire, water, earth, and air.

The basic emotions of grief, anger, apathy, and fear each correspond to water, fire, earth, and air respectively. You are constitutionally prone to certain emotions based on your elemental profile. If you have a strong fire element, you are likely to be vibrant and charismatic, but quick to anger and seek recognition. Water element folks tend to be highly perceptive, introverted, and self-affirming, but can be overly emotional and prone to depression. Earth element people are patient, kind, and nurturing, but on the other hand they can be stubborn, fixed in their ways, and disposed to complacency and laziness. Being aware of your own natural tendency enables you to have a different perspective and perhaps even some levity when your elements start acting up.

In my book *Happily Ever After,* I speak in more detail about the natural elements and the related love and success blocks, as well as common beliefs of each element. More information, including a free natural assessment, is available at my website: www.sukisohn.com/what-is-your-love-block.

EXERCISE: Healing Emotions through Healing the Elements

The body also needs to be balanced. Throughout the world's ancient healing practices ranging from Greece and India to China, it was believed that the body is composed of natural elements. The actual elements vary from culture to culture. Seeing the gap in each of these systems, I have integrated the various elements to create the 7 Elements System: water, earth, fire, air, wood, metal, and spirit. When the elements of the body are unbalanced, our thoughts, emotions, and body are not at ease.

Each element has an emotional aspect.

The spirit element is related to the sense of the divine and the Other World. It is the element that gives us perspective and a sense of connection to something greater than our singular lives. An imbalance of spirit will cause us to feel insignificant, limited, and, in extremes, ignorant and closed-minded.

The air element is associated with communication, cleverness, and a sense of levity. When the air element is out of balance, you tend to be flighty, nervous, and easily agitated. The fire element instills charisma, passion, and willpower, and gives you a sense of inspiration. When it is out of balance one is easily angered, impulsive, and hot-headed. A healthy water element brings serenity and calms your emotions. It also gives rise to intuition and insight. Otherwise, an out of balance water element may make you feel overly sensitive or emotionally turbulent. The healthy earth element allows you to feel grounded and safe. It also gives rise to nurturing qualities. When out of balance, earth makes us stubborn, resistant to needed change, smothering, and emotionally needy. Wood element, when in balance, brings ambition, expansiveness, an adventurous spirit, and generosity; while out of balance the wood element causes us to be insensitive workaholics and impatient. The metal element in balance brings a clear, logical mind, precision, organization, resilience, and simple elegance; while out of balance the metal causes us to be overly critical of ourselves and others. Their words can be also sharp and cutting.

In the Healing the Elements practice, we learn to visualize and work with the energies that affect the balance of these elements.

1. Visualize colored light streaming forth from a deity of your choice. Jesus, Buddha, Virgin Mary, or Isis. It does not matter as long as you have an emotional connection with them. If you are an atheist, visualize a ball of energy of the primordial life force in front of you.

2. The rays emanating renew each of our elements with the essence of inexhaustible vitality.

3. We associate a golden light with the earth element. A white, opalescent light is associated with the spirit element. The fire element is red-orange, like the glow of molten metal. The air element is sky blue, and the metal element is silver. The wood element is emerald green and the water element is deep blue.

4. We visualize these colors streaming forth from your deity of choice.

5. The light of each element extends to the outermost reaches of the universe and collects the essence of each element.

6. Then we visualize this light and similarly-colored liquid completely filling our bodies and fully rejuvenating each of our elements in turn.

To download an audio version of this exercise, please visit my website at: www.sukisohn.com/resources.

CHAPTER 8

Power of Magnetism

In Chapter 7, we learned how that thought, the masculine aspect, creates an electric charge and then, through a chemical reaction, emotion and a magnetic charge are created. Combined they create an electromagnetic field. This field can expand and contract depending on your state of being and it can also attract and repel those around you.

On a practical level, who are the people that you are naturally drawn to and want to be around? What is their "vibe" and how do they make you feel? People who are naturally magnetic are those who vibrate levels of consciousness that are 200 and above. When you are vibrating at the level of shame, guilt, grief, and despair, you are unconsciously repelling those around you. When you are feeling these kinds of emotions, you are also less likely to be around other people. You are likely to feel tense, anxious, contracted, and will be exuding this quality.

Heart Rhythm and Magnetism

According to the studies conducted by the HeartMath Institute, a person's emotional state is encoded in the magnetic field generated by the heart:

We have found there is a direct relationship between the heart-rhythm patterns and the spectral information encoded in the frequency spectra of the magnetic field radiated by the heart. Thus, information about a person's emotional state is encoded in the heart's magnetic field and is communicated throughout the body and into the external environment.

Most people tend to think of communication solely in terms of overt signals expressed through facial movements, voice qualities, gestures, and body movements. However, evidence now supports the perspective that a subtle yet influential electromagnetic or "energetic" communication system operates just below our conscious level of awareness.

Below, Figure 2 shows the ECG data during two different emotional states – heartfelt gratitude and anger. According to this study, the human body has various means for detecting its external stimuli beyond the obvious five senses.

Most people believe that communication is solely based on overt signals expressed through facial movements, voice qualities, gestures, and body movements. However, evidence now supports the perspective that a subtle yet influential electromagnetic or "energetic" communication system operates just below our conscious level of awareness. Data suggest that this energetic system contributes to the "magnetic" attractions or repulsions that occur between individuals.

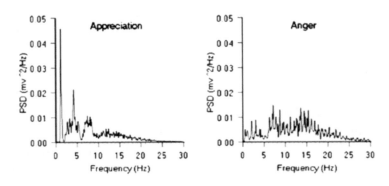

Figure 2: ECG Spectra during different emotional states.
Source: HeartMath Institute, Science of the Heart Volume 2, 2015

The HeartMath Institute study shows that the magnetic field created by the heart can be detected several feet away. They have also found evidence that the magnetic signals radiated by the heart can affect the brain rhythms of another.

The heart is thus responsible for sending out intangible signals to attract or repel those around us. Most people are unconscious of the "vibes" they are sending out nor are they aware of how their own emotions are influencing or distorting their thoughts. The HeartMath Institute also stated that coherent heart rhythms enable you to be more empathic while maintaining internal stability.

Magnetism Comes from a State of Being

Magnetic force does not physically disrupt the object it attracts or repels. In contrast, electric force penetrates and disrupts the object it interacts with. Relating this metaphor to human behavior, this contrast can be seen as a "state of being" vs. a "state of doing." Modern society encourages and promotes doing over a state of being. Of course, both are needed for the successful outcome of any situation. However, there is no doubt that we as society suffer from the frantic pace of do, do, do. Even when you seem to be passive, like binge-watching Netflix, you are in a state of doing, being affected by external stimuli. We have very little time in which we are just fully and simply present in the moment. When the opportunity arises to be simply present, we get bored and try to fill that time with an activity, like perusing social media, instead of gazing out the window.

My emphasis on "being-ness" may be mistakenly interpreted as being passive or lazy, but nothing could be further from the truth. A good metaphor would be being a good listener rather than being the one that constantly dominates the conversation. A state of being is a state of awareness and when you are in a state of being, your heart is awake.

When the heart is awake, things come to you with what seems like little effort. On a metaphysical level, the expansive and magnetic nature of the heart does indeed attract to you what you desire. On a practical level, when our heart is open our perception of reality changes. An open heart is grateful, fluid, affable, and equanimous. When you have an open heart and your heart's desire is clear, your efforts toward achieving your goals become pleasurable, which creates the perception that things came easily – because they did!

Magnetism and the Quantum Field

The quantum aspect of magnetism can be explained through the Double Slit Experiment and the Observer Effect. This famous experiment shows that quantum, which is defined *as the smallest possible discrete unit of any physical property, such as energy or matter,* behaves differently depending on the expectations of the observer. When there was no observer, the quantum photons behaved liked waves, i.e. carried the possibility of many potential outcomes. However, when observed, they acted like discrete physical matter, collapsing into only one possibility of being, as expected by the observer.

You are the observer and creator of your life. You are the one that collapses all the quantum possibilities to a single outcome based on your thoughts and emotions. You are the one influencing the quantum field around you. You magnetize the frequency that you put out. If you send out the frequency of forgiveness, compassion, love, and abundance, that is what you will magnetize by resonance. As Einstein said: *"Everything is energy and that's all there is to it. Match the frequency of the reality you want, and you cannot help but get that reality. It can be no other way. This is not philosophy. This is physics."*

Lessons of the Spider

The lesson of magnetism came to me while watching a spider in my garden. This little spider created an optimal circumstance by building her intricate web at a spot where a gentle breeze could deliver her prey. Once she completed her web ("doing"), she hid in a corner and patiently waited ("being"). She did not chase her prey, her prey came to her. How many times in your life have you desperately grasped and clawed at things?

I see this often in my clients when they meet someone they are interested in. I call it "decorating the nursery." Before even getting a chance to figure out whether the person is someone they want to be with long term, they get attached. But the nature of this attachment is about control, not connection.

Judy was a type-A ball-buster senior executive at a large pharmaceutical company. She was in her later thirties and was looking to meet the *one*. She had a few serious relationships but for the last few years she was going through a dry spell. She met Ralph at work. He was a consultant brought in to train senior executives on communication skills. She was immediately drawn to his intelligence and poise. After their initial meeting, he reached out to her via email and she was flattered and intrigued.

After a few email exchanges, they agreed to meet. However, when the day came around for them to meet, he completely went radio silent and did not respond to her emails. She felt humiliated and angry. She obsessed over Ralph, analyzing the situation over and over again, trying to understand what had happened. By chance, Judy bumped into him at a random social event. Ralph casually commented on his not responding to emails, which sent Judy into an emotional tailspin. She tried to play cool, but she was shaken and spent the next few days expending way too much energy over the situation.

At work and in different areas of her personal growth, when Judy wanted something she went for it full on. She did her best to anticipate all possible circumstances and made consistent and disciplined efforts to reach her goals. Her forcefulness and determination allowed her to have a sense of control over her life. Unfortunately, when it comes to matters of the heart resonance and relating to men, this type of grasping behavior often backfires. The lesson she needed to learn was to let her love interests come to her instead of chasing after them. This was a hard lesson for her to learn, because it went against her natural assertive proactive nature.

When you take a deeper look at grasping behavior, there is always a feeling of insecurity or lack. Many successful professionals are motivated by this sense of not being enough and lack, and as a result go to immense measures to compensate for their perceived shortcomings. In other words, they try too hard. In order to cultivate magnetism you must learn to have the patience of the spider.

Control Repels, Surrender Attracts

Have you ever tried to grab a beach ball floating in a pool? You will notice if you rush toward it, the ripple your rushed movement creates pushes the ball away further. If you lunge toward it, the ball will most likely pop right out of your grasp. Magnetism asks you to slow down to go fast. A direct, active, and forceful approach is more often than *not* the best course of action.

Beth had been trying to get pregnant for a number of years. She went through a number of failed IVF attempts and was starting to get discouraged. She was an avid athlete and didn't miss a beat. She was in incredible shape, yet there was a tightness and hardness about her. If you ever had a cat, you probably noticed their agility and grace. They have powerful muscles that allow them to jump many times their height, yet when they are relaxed their muscles are completely soft and supple.

Beth did not know how to relax. She was always on the go. There was neither softness nor an ability to relax and receive in her for a baby to take hold. She also held beliefs that the baby would restrict her freedom. She didn't realize she was unconsciously rejecting getting pregnant.

The beach ball metaphor was an epiphany for her. She cut down on her athletic regime and learned how to slow down and, like magic, her following IVF treatment resulted in a beautiful baby girl.

Sexual Magnetism and Polarity

David Deida, tantra teacher and expert on sexuality, states:

> Sexual attraction is based upon sexual polarity, which is the force of passion that arcs between the masculine and feminine poles thus creating the flow of sexual feeling. If you want real passion you need a ravisher and a ravishee, otherwise you just have two buddies who rub genitals in bed….The love may still be strong, the friendship may still be strong, but the sexual polarity fades unless in moments of intimacy one

partner is willing to play the masculine pole and one partner is willing to play the feminine. You have to animate the masculine and the feminine differences if you want to play in the field of sexual passion.

He further defines femininity and masculinity in the following way:

CORE MASCULINE TRAITS	CORE FEMININE TRAITS
Sense of mission leading to freedom	The search for love and intimacy
Competitive	Compassionate
Living on the edge	Deep, radiant beauty
Analytical	Emotional
Growth from challenge	Growth from support and praise
Definitive and decisive	Subtle and unpredictable

When I first encountered his book *The Way of the Superior Man*, my first reaction was to be offended. I strongly identified with many of the core masculine traits and so would many of my clients. However, experience has taught me that there is no denying the simple truth that passion and sexual attraction do require this polarity. In a trusting relationship, these gender roles can be fluid. However, initially, the core instinct of man would be to feel jeopardized if a woman in his life consistently took on masculine traits. This would trigger the natural "masculine" competitive tendencies, which is truly the last thing you want in a romantic relationship.

Beauty of Receptivity

How well are you able to receive love, praise, and attention? Do you blush or become tense? You may not express this outwardly, but how do you feel inside when someone gives you a sincere compliment? When someone wants to ravish you and worship you, can you truly take it all in?

When you are able to gracefully and gratefully receive, you are sending a message to those around you and the Universe that you would like more of whatever is given. However, if it makes you uncomfortable and you unconsciously energetically repel these gifts, they will most likely start disappearing from your life.

The Taoist mind-body practice of accumulating *chi, life force energy,* understood that there is energy all around us. It is our job to magnetize and be receptive, through creating space, an emptiness, and a sense of surrender within, to fully receive the blessings around us.

Ask yourself, are you one who believes life is suffering and that you have to fight for everything? If you believe this, your life will be so. However, if you believe that life is a gift and that love, blessings, beauty, and energy are all around us and that all you have to do is be truly and gratefully open to it, then your life will be just so. This isn't about manifesting. This is actually about shifting perspectives that can quickly liberate you from the prison you created for yourself. Unlike manifesting, which often takes some time, the gifts from shifting your perspective are instantaneous.

Another belief that holds you back from being receptive could be a sense of not being worthy or, in some high-achieving women, the belief you have to work hard to be worthy. And if you feel that you have not sufficiently paid your dues, then your sense of guilt leads to a feeling of not being worthy.

I will let you in on a secret. If you are not worthy, you will not be receiving the attention and energy coming your way. If it's coming your way, you deserve it, so revel in it. Take it all in. Be grateful for it. This way you will magnetize more of it.

How to Develop Magnetism

Recapping what we have discussed, there are five keys to developing magnetism:

Let Go of Attachments

Attachments prevent you from receiving, as you block energy coming your way with your attachments. This does not mean you do not have dreams or goals. When I pray or desire to manifest something, I always add, "or something better." The Universe may be trying to send you something better, or something better for you, than what you wished for.

Emanate the Frequency You Wish to Attract

As Einstein said: "Everything is energy and that's all there is
to it. Match the frequency of the reality you want, and you
cannot help but get that reality. It can be no other way. This is
not philosophy. This is physics." You magnetize the frequency
you put out. Be mindful of what energies and beliefs you are
vibrating. If you are suspicious, judgmental, lack-focused,
and closed, you are sending a signal to the Universe that you
are not ready to receive, and you will receive more of what
you resonate – lack, judgment, and doubt. Gratitude, trust,
openness, and kindness are the frequencies you want to emit
to attract the love and life you desire.

Create Congruency

Every part of you is there to serve you, even your inner
critic. Your heart and brain may not be in sync, leading to
sending a confusing message to the Universe. Like Beth,
who consciously wanted a baby but deep down held a belief
that a baby would limit her freedom, conflicting beliefs need
to be cleared to magnetize the outcome you desire.

Cultivate Your Ability to Receive

When praise, love, and attention comes your way, practice
receiving them graciously with a smile and sincere gratitude.
Know that if it's coming your way, you deserve it. The

Universe is abundant and always providing that which you desire most. Inability to receive and thus repelling, judging, or dismissing gifts will stop the flow.

Understand and Work with the Laws of Polarity

There is no point denying that magnetism is based on the Laws of Polarity. There must be negative and positive, giver and receiver, feminine and masculine for magnetic force to take effect. Examine what role you naturally play.

EXERCISE: Magnetizing in the Quantum Field

Magnetizing requires embodying and "being." The following exercise guides you to absorb your dreams into your being to manifest them into your life:

1. Identify a wish, dream, or desire you want to manifest that comes from the depth of your soul. Make sure it is truly a dream, not a "nice-to-have" or a mere fantasy.

2. Take a deep breath and, as you exhale, close your eyes to see a very black space or void. I call this place the primordial abyss, a space of infinite potential, yet nothing has manifested yet, like the universe before the big bang.

3. In this void, watch a luminescent light, a star, appear.

4. Project your dream into the star. Watch the star as it absorbs your dream.

5. Magnetize or pull the star toward you and draw it into your forehead. Watch the third eye (the space slightly above your eyebrows) absorb the star.

6. Envision the inside of your head as a crystal ball or a globe of mirrors. The dream star is now reflected and magnified throughout this crystal palace.

7. Watch the dream star explode three times, but instead of being destroyed, it is energized and shines more brilliantly. Imagine the expanding universe after the big bang.

8. Watch the energy generated from the explosions penetrate the cells in your brain and become deeply integrated into your mind.

9. Now let the energy float or permeate down to your heart. See that your heart also has a crystal palace reflecting and magnifying the dream star.

10. Again, watch the dream and star explode three times. With each explosion, feel your heart affirming and committing to making this dream a reality.

11. Feel the sensation in your body produced by the merging of the energy of the dream star with your heart.

12. Once the heart is completely full with this energy, watch it descend further into your lower abdomen into your womb (or a similar position, if you are a man). Again, the inside of your womb is a crystal palace reflecting and magnifying the dream star.

13. The dream star explodes three times, penetrating your lower abdomen with the energy.

14. Feel the excitement and passion arising from your lower abdomen in its alignment with your dream.

15. Finally, the let energy flow through your pelvis down your legs into the soles of your feet and then deep into the molten core of Mother Earth.

16. As the dream star touches the core of the earth, watch it explode once again, this time creating a huge burst of energy fed by Mother Earth back into your body, up your head, and straight up into the void, creating a beacon or pillar of light through you.

17. Feel the powerful energy flow through you.

18. When you are ready, take a deep breath and, as you exhale, open your eyes.

For an audio recording of this exercise, please visit: www.sukisohn.com/resources.

CHAPTER 9

Power of Intuition

When the time of our ordinary mind stops, we enter the time of Spirit, the sacred time, the time when everything is possible.

— Arkan Lushwala

In this chapter we will explore the nature of intuition and how to cultivate it. Intuition is a crucial part of our ability to make any kind of decision. Women's natural empathic abilities generally make it easier to tap into this sacred gift.

Heart Intelligence and Intuition

In addition to the heart's ability to attract and repel through the frequency encoded in its magnetic field, the heart is also the source of your intuition. Studies by the HeartMath Institute have shown that the heart's abilities are not bound by time and space, as it has the uncanny ability to react to future events before the event even takes place:

> *Heart intelligence is the flow of higher awareness and the intuition we experience when the mind and emotions are brought into synchronistic alignment with the energetic heart. When we are heart-centered and coherent, we have a tighter coupling and closer alignment with our deeper source of intuitive intelligence. We are able to more intelligently self-regulate our thoughts and emotions and over time this lifts consciousness and establishes a new internal physiological and psychological baseline. In other words, there is an increased flow of intuitive information that is communicated via the emotional energetic system to the mind and brain systems, resulting in a stronger connection with our deeper inner voice.*

Intuition is the primary source of decision-making. Whether that decision is about who to go on a date with or what stocks to purchase, decisions are made by the unconscious mind. Studies have shown that there is a spike in brain activity seconds prior to the moment that the subject is consciously aware that she has made a decision.[6] And according to HeartMath Institute, the heart reacts seconds faster than the brain.

Stargate Research

It is now public knowledge that in 1978 the CIA established a US Army unit, the Stargate Project, to investigate the potential use of psychic powers for its intelligence operations. The Stargate Project primarily looked into remote viewing, the ability to see events and sites from a great distance. The Project was terminated in 1995 after a report concluded that the information gathered was either too vague, irrelevant, or erroneous.

The research at the HeartMath Institute showed that in order to increase the heart's intelligence, i.e. its intuitive abilities, that "the mind and emotions [need to be] brought into synchronistic alignment with the energetic heart." Here they are describing a state of high heart-brain coherency. In layperson's terms, the mind and heart are aligned, calm, and at ease. I cannot imagine that the CIA investigation had a chance at really understanding the potential of these abilities without considering the subtle emotional factors of the subjects they were studying. The idea of using intuitive powers for military use itself seems to be incongruent with the heart's natural preference for compassion and empathy.

Validating Intuition

When I first heard of these kinds of abilities I was skeptical, but I decided to keep an open mind and see what my intuition could offer. During one exercise, I was asked to "remote view" and scan what health problems, if any, a couple was experiencing. Their names and the fact that they lived in Argentina were the only information given to me. When I scanned their bodies, I saw, or had a knowing, that the couple was an elderly couple. The wife had trouble with her thyroid and she had metastasized cancer. Her husband was generally healthy but suffered from back and joint pain. I was amazed to hear that I had "guessed" accurately. I thought, *Well, this could be coincidence*, but I continued to have experiences like this.

On another occasion, I was able to detect in a client what I saw as an electrical glitch in the brain and that she needed a small dose of medication to stabilize the situation. Of course, I would never diagnose a client or recommend any medical course of action; however, I did guide her to seek professional medical help.

Intuition is a birthright of humanity and everyone has the ability to develop supernatural intuitive abilities. Unfortunately, modern society does not honor nor help cultivate intuition. Einstein said that he never made any of his discoveries through rational thinking, and he went as far as to say that the only really valuable thing is intuition.

Three Types of Inner Knowing

Intuition is a feminine gift, though there are of course many men with powerful intuitive abilities. The men, particularly shamans and healers, who I have met with these abilities have all, without exception, honored the divine feminine with deep reverence. A woman's natural empathic abilities give her an edge when it comes to cultivating these gifts. There are subtle differences to the kind of supernatural inner knowing – insight, intuition, and instinct. The three are related to the head-brain, heart-brain, and the gut-brain.

Neuroscientists have discovered that the heart and gut have an extensive network of neurons and synaptic nerves that make decisions independent of the head-brain. The head-brain is where insight arises, the heart-brain is where intuition arises, and gut-brain is where instinct arises. We will explore the function of the three brains in the following chapter, but here I would like to discuss the connection between the three brains and the three types of inner knowing.

Instinct is defined by the *Merriam-Webster Dictionary* as, "*a largely inheritable and unalterable tendency of an organism to make a complex and specific response to environmental stimuli without involving reason.*" Instinct is, in short, a response to external stimuli and is largely to do with the feelings of threat or safety. The emotions associated with instinct are fear or pleasure and attraction.

Intuition is defined as, *"the power or faculty of attaining to direct knowledge or cognition without evident rational thought and inference."* Intuition does not require an external stimulus. It is self-arising from the heart, though we may feel an emotional and physical response.

Insight is defined as, *"the act or result of apprehending the inner nature of things."* Unlike instinct and intuition, there is no emotional quality to insight. Insight is where you are able to see beyond the surface appearance of things and understand the mysterious machination of metaphysical phenomenon behind the physical manifestations.

Honoring Imagination

The first step to cultivating inner knowing is imagination. Einstein said that logic can get us from A to Z but imagination can take us anywhere. The logical, empirical mind cannot make sense of inner knowing as it cannot track, at least not yet, how the "information" that inner knowing provides arises. So, its first tendency is to dismiss it. Imagination is the gateway to a higher knowing. It is what allows us to perceive beyond our predictable norm outside of empirical observations.

Imagination is what expands the mind beyond the ordinary run of the mill thoughts. It is the seed of all creativity and innovation. The ordinary stay ordinary because they are unable to harness the power of imagination.

Imagination unlocks the limitations of the logical mind to the realm of inner knowing out of which arises the Universal Consciousness.

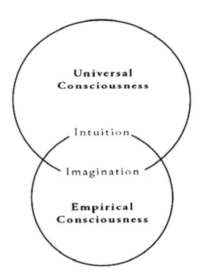

I am bemused when clients say, "Well I just made that up." I ask them, "Really? Where did you make it up from?" Imagination stands guard at the border of where your logical and ego-based mind meets the Universal Consciousness, the source of inner knowing. Only those able to surrender the limits of the logical mind through imagination are worthy to access the depth of wisdom of the Universal Consciousness.

Premonitions, Signs, and Synchronicity

Whether you had given it any more energy than a passing thought or carefully studied its meanings, I am sure you have all experienced intriguing synchronicities, had premonitions, and recognized signs in your life. We are connected to the universe around us in ways that we can only begin to imagine. Every single cell in our bodies is constantly in reaction with our environment and is as a result able to witness various signals that are beyond logic.

Jill Bolte Taylor was a brain scientist who, through a stroke, temporarily lost the functions of her left brain, which is the part of our brain that operates in fixed time and space, is logical, and focuses on the visible physical phenomenon. In her book, she recounts her insights from her experience:

> Based upon my experience with losing my left mind, I whole-heartedly believe that the feeling of deep inner peace is neurological circuitry located in our right brain. Our right brain perceives the big picture and recognizes that everything around us, about us, among us and within us is made up of energy particles that are woven together into a universal tapestry. Since everything is connected, there is an intimate relationship between the atomic space around and within me, and the atomic space around and within you – regardless of where we are…. And I

must say, there was both freedom and challenge
for me in recognizing that our perception of
the external world, and our relationship to it, is
a product of our neurological circuitry. For all
those years of my life, I really had been a figment
of my own imagination

While the left brain's primary function is language, logic, and singularity, the masculine brain, the right brain is the place of mystery, connectivity, and inner knowing, the feminine brain. The right brain communicates in images rather than words. Increasing our ability to recognize important premonitions, signs, and symbols is largely associated with our ability to utilize the right brain. Because the right brain is not linear or logical, you must access it via your emotions and bodily sensations to unearth the wisdom that it brings to our lives.

Penetrating the Brain to Access Supernatural Abilities

There are three functions of the human brain – mental, emotional, and physical. The prefrontal cortex responds to the logical thinking brain, the limbic system controls the emotions, and finally the cerebellum, a.k.a. life brain, regulates life functions related to our very survival, such as breathing and metabolic functions. The life brain is the part of us that is connected to supernatural human abilities. Wim

Hof mastered yogic breath that allows him to withstand arctic temperatures in a pair of running shorts, earning his nickname the Iceman.[7] Penetrating the levels of the brain is not an easy task.

Between the prefrontal cortex and the limbic system, i.e. the thinking brain and the emotional, lay doubt and judgment. Doubt about one's abilities or skepticism often stops our attempts to expand beyond our comfort zone. Then, between the limbic system and the life brain lies fear – the fear of change, the fear of our own powers, and many other irrational fears may arise.

Though the awareness of these natural tendencies gives us an edge, it does not preclude us from having to exert considerable and dedicated effort to gain extraordinary abilities, not because it's inaccessible but rather because our habitual thinking is so entrenched.

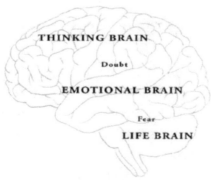

Figure 3: Three Layers of the Brain

How to Cultivate Intuition

In order to clear the channels so you can hear the subtle voice of inner knowing, there are few principles to understand and follow. First, cultivate a state where your heart and brain are congruent, i.e. aligned. When your head is saying one thing and your heart another, the chatter caused by the conflict will not allow you to be open to the quiet voice of intuition. Second, have no agenda or attachment to any outcome. This is very difficult to achieve if we have strong desires one way or another. However, this internal bias will distort our ability to see clearly what is in front of us. Third, honor your imagination! Modern society devalues imagination to child's play. However, imagination is the key to the wisdom of your right brain. Imagination allows us to expand beyond logic. Finally, validate your intuition. I mean that in both senses of the word. Validate your intuition through tracking it to see what eventually comes about. When I was testing my intuition as a medical intuitive, I constantly cross-referenced my visions with medical texts and research. Also, validate and encourage yourself. Your intuition will continue to elevate if you continue to use this muscle and consistently validate it.

ନ୍ଥ

EXERCISE: Developing Soft Vision

Inner knowing comes from a soft diffused focus that allows us to more widely absorb the information around us. For most of the waking parts of the day, we are in a narrow focus and a beta brainwave. In order to tap into inner knowing we need to learn to develop a soft focus which allows for an opening of sorts. Here is a simple exercise to start cultivating this holistic way of sensing the world around us by developing and expanding upon our natural proprioception.[8]

1. Bring your attention to an object in front of you.

2. Notice how your vision is focused on this object, though you can see more through your peripheral vision.

3. Now expand your vision from that object and soften your focus so that you can give equal energy to your peripheral vision.

4. Now expand beyond your peripheral vision to behind you, above you, and then below you.

5. Notice what sensations you feel in your body and what awareness arises as you continue to hold your vision soft and expansive.

It is good to do this exercise in nature, as when you are able to open up to your sixth sense through this exercise, you will notice that nature has a lot say when you are ready to listen.

CHAPTER 10

Power of Nurturance

Nothing is so strong as gentleness, nothing so gentle as real strength.

– Saint Francis de Sales

Allison was a successful serial entrepreneur. She was well-respected in her field and her passion and energy were inspiring to be around. I stated in Chapter 3 that the masculine is inspiring while the feminine is nurturing. Allison's first start-up was sold to a strategic investor after four years. However, shortly after the sale, she was asked to leave as the new management felt that she didn't have the right profile for the job. She was heartbroken and upset by the departure, though she was financially well rewarded.

Though she had the forceful nature to create momentum from nothing, she lacked the ability to nurture and sustain. After a year sabbatical, she started a new company, this time on her own. Her new challenge was hiring and maintaining quality staff. It seemed that she was either hiring the wrong people or she seemed to be unable to hold on to good people.

This was also reflected in her personal relationships. Despite the fact that she was tired of the dating scene and wanted to find someone to share her life with, she was constantly juggling and dating multiple guys. Each new person she met she thought was the one, only to lead to disappointment after disappointment. People with the fire element out of balance experience these kinds of challenges.

The power of nurturance lies in a sincere, steady, and constant level of attention. Unlike the element of fire, which is proud, flamboyant, and loves to be seen, nurturing comes from the earth element. Think of the plants and trees that grow from earth. This energy is not rushed or "showy." In fact, it almost seems imperceptible. Shannon, a former colleague of mine, was a good example of someone who exhibited the power of nurturance. She was the CFO of her company and was respected by her team, peers, and superiors. She was steady, dependable, and fair. She only spoke when necessary, but when she did people listened. She didn't have the kind of charisma that Allison had, but there was a gravitas about her that you could not ignore. When Shannon requested something she got it, no argument.

True Nurturance

I often meet clients with a misguided view of nurturing. They often come with the story and belief that they have to be nice to be liked. Often, they are not even conscious that they hold this belief. As a result, they go out of their way to help and please others, emptying their own tank in the process. This type of "nurturing" inevitably leads to guilt on the part of receiver and resentment on the part of the giver. Allison, who seemed like a powerful and independent woman, was truthfully empty inside. Her attention was constantly outward, wondering how she would be perceived by others.

The power of nurturance is cultivated when you nurture yourself first. Your ability to care for others is rooted in your ability to care for yourself. You must be full of love, regard, and compassion for yourself before it can overflow and radiate from you. Playing the woeful martyr is not feminine. That is simply either a sign of low self-esteem or a ploy to manipulate or both. Stop tending other people's gardens when yours is overrun with weeds.

Compassionate Pruning

If you have any experience with gardening, you will know that thoughtful and consistent pruning is necessary to help your garden to thrive. Relationships are no different. Part of nurturing is to create clear boundaries and expectations, and communicate them to your partner. Being the nurturing feminine is not only about gentle support but sometimes a quick well-considered cut is what is needed. However, this must be done from compassion that allows for neutrality and clear vision.

When your tank is empty, it is very likely that you will be swept up in emotions and are more likely to lash out blindly, damaging the relationship. Shannon had the incredible ability to give feedback in a manner that was always fair and neutral. When she spoke, her assessments on areas of improvement were kind but surgical and impartial.

Receptivity and Nurturance

Nurturing does not always have to be an act of giving. Sometimes nurturing can be genuine receiving. Sometimes a simple smile of gratitude can be the most nurturing thing for the person who offered you a gift.

In sexual relationships, when a man is truly in love, he will more likely be interested in your pleasure over his own. If you are unable to receive his passion and ardor, imagine how that would make him feel. Rejected and unappreciated? You bet!

Genuine and complete receiving is a gift and the best possible expression of gratitude to the one who gave it to you.

The Three Brains

When we think of the brain, most people only think of the head-brain, but neuroscientists have now discovered that there is a complex network of neurons and synaptic nerves that make decisions independent of the head-brain in our body – specifically the heart and gut. The Taoist knew this and called these the three energy centers – Upper Palace for your brain, Middle Palace for your heart, and Lower Palace for your gut – and had developed extensive mind-body trainings to cultivate and align the three brains.

The brain-led person (a masculine mode) is super-logical and always thinking. They are often disassociated with their emotions to the point that if you ask them the question, "How do you feel?" they often answer with "I think." These are the strategists and tacticians. The head-brain's primary function is to figure out *how* to do things. Strong metal element people fall into this category.

The gut-based person is another example of the masculine mode. They are gutsy, bold, and courageous. The warrior culture and ethos would fall in this category. The gut brain is what creates the energy and passion to move forward in spite of fear, obstacles, and challenges. This is where you find the *will* to do things. The fire and wood elements are often the warrior types.

Finally, the heart-based person – the typical feminine mode – is primarily focused on how they connect with other people. The heart is where the *why* is found. This is where your personal values lie and what truly gives *meaning* to anything you do.

If you are human, you have all three brains, but we typically have a default pattern.

Most corporate executives, both men and women, fall into the head-based person where they lead with their brain and drum up the willpower to do it with very little regard to the heart. Entrepreneurs typically lead with the gut. They will just get started with gusto and figure out how along the way. Again, many of them fail to check in with why they are doing what they are doing.

I am a huge fan of Simon Sinek's work *Start with Why*. Despite his success as entrepreneur, he found himself broken and demotivated – precisely because he lost his why. I would say he lost his heart, that is, his feminine aspect. Steven Pressfield, ex-marine and author of the *Warrior Ethos* begins his book on the warrior mindset with two chapters about the feminine. Both authors would agree that the feminine aspect, the heart, comes first and you fail to do so at your own peril.

A heart-based person is one who honors and cultivates the power of nurturance. When you are led by your heart, your three brains naturally come into alignment. But how do you know when your brain is in alignment? Do you recall that feeling you get when you are touched and moved by something? That good lump in your throat that almost moves you to tears? That is when your Vagus nerve is activated. The Vagus nerve connects the three brains and when it is flowing freely it activates a feeling of expansiveness, euphoria, gratitude, and sometimes a sense of awe and sacredness in everything around us. When your three brains are aligned, your masculine and feminine are in balance, allowing the best of you to emerge.

EXERCISE: Creating an Altar, Your Inner Garden

There are many ways to "tend your garden," i.e. self-care. Meditation, going to the gym, a warm bath, dancing, gardening, and spending time doing things you love to do are all great ways to "fill your tank." But the most powerful method that allowed me to create my own inner space was setting up an altar that I maintained daily.

For some this may seem too religious and nearing idol worship. However, creating an altar allows you to cultivate a relationship with yourself through nurturing a relationship with a representational deity. This deity is actually you, the highest, best, and most evolved form of you. What you offer to this deity is what you offer yourself.

I set up a small area where I spend time meditating, practicing yoga, or simply contemplating. Below is a quick guideline to my offerings, which are based on a Tibetan Buddhist altar, but you can create your own. The only guideline or intention is to offer all that you desire in your life.

My altar consists of:

- Statues or images of deities, angels, buddhas
- Fragrant flowers
- Clean drinking water
- Clean washing water
- Incense
- Candle
- Perfumed water
- Food (non-perishables like nuts, dried fruits, or chocolate)
- Musical instrument

I have had a meditation practice for some time but creating my altar solidified and grounded my practice. Now I feel like missing my daily practice is standing up my chosen deity and my higher self.

CHAPTER 11

Power of Interdependence

Growing up I had a challenging relationship with my mother. I was a rambunctious, hyper-energetic, and passionately opinionated little girl. Now being a parent, I can see how challenging it must have been for my mother to raise me. I certainly was a handful! But in my little mind at the time, I believed that my mother favored my sister over me.

My sister was the good little girl who was quiet and obedient. In many of my heated arguments with my mother which ended up in me in tears locked in my bedroom, I told myself I didn't need her. I didn't need anyone. I said this over and over like a mantra. The anger and sadness that I felt feeling rejected from my mother I channeled into becoming independent on all fronts.

My divorce with my first husband only compounded this belief. I never wanted to be in the position where I needed someone and this need for independence made me strong, self-motivated, and self-reliant.

Now married with two kids, I became aware of how this *need* for independence created a subtle and invisible wall between me and my husband, kids, and friends. I am there when they need me, and I am happy to play this role. But to admit at any level that I need them? I could not bear to say "I need you" to anyone. I always wanted to be the one who was needed. This kept me safe.

One fateful day, I said to my husband, "I need you." I have said: I love you, I adore you, I care for you etc. a million times, but, "I need you?" I never voiced those words to anyone in my life! Saying these words created a whirlwind of emotions, including self-hatred! Yet at the same time I realized I was giving my husband a gift – the gift of my vulnerability and trust.

Hiding behind spirituality, I told myself that I only needed the love of God (the Creator of all that is), since humans no matter how well-intentioned can disappoint you. What I didn't realize is that God shows up in my life through my husband, children, family and friends, strangers, serendipitous events, and chance connections.

My independence and self-reliance served me well at work, but I now realize that I *need* the emotional support and love from my husband, joy and laughter of my children, the community and perspective from my friends, and even the inspiration I get from chance encounters with strangers. Just like taking a business to another level forces solopreneurs to build a team, I realized it was time to trade independence for interdependence. Maturing into a model of healthy interdependence from independence, or in some cases co-dependence, is one of the key aspects of empowered femininity.

Are you perhaps suffering from a self-imposed isolation of independence, always there for others but unable to ask or accept help from others? As much as I love Wonder Woman, would you like to live her life of isolation, always being the untouchable savior?

Holistic Perspective of Interdependence

All things animate or inanimate are connected in an intricate web of interdependence. The idea that we are distinct or separate from the universe around us is an illusion. A narrow perspective of self in relation to other promotes an unhealthy overly-competitive culture where nobody truly wins.

As we discussed previously, women's brains are thus more apt to see the connectivity of all things, and perhaps this is one reason why men sometimes find women ambiguous.

The masculine aspect thrives and seeks out competition for growth while the feminine flourishes with support and exchange. The competitive view of the world without the balance of the feminine is limiting and necessarily leads to a zero-sum game of someone losing out. The power of interdependence lies in that it recognizes that we are all connected and that there is a way to all come out on top.

I love the African concept of *Ubuntu* instilled in children from a young age. It translates to "I am what I am because of who we all are." It is a traditional African philosophy that offers us an understanding of ourselves in relation with the world and this philosophy is shared by many other pre-religion indigenous spiritual cultures that lived close to nature. Nobel Laureate Archbishop Desmond Tutu describes Ubuntu as:

> *It is the essence of being human. It speaks of the fact that my humanity is caught up and is inextricably bound up in yours. I am human because I belong. It speaks about wholeness, it speaks about compassion. A person with Ubuntu is welcoming, hospitable, warm, and generous, willing to share. Such people are open and available to others, willing to be vulnerable, affirming of others, do not feel threatened that others are able and good, for they have a proper self-assurance that comes from knowing that they belong in a greater whole. They know that they are diminished when others are humiliated, diminished when others are oppressed,*

diminished when others are treated as if they were less than who they are. The quality of Ubuntu gives people resilience, enabling them to survive and emerge still human despite all efforts to dehumanize them.

This view is shared with Einstein, who said:

A human being is a part of the whole called by us universe, a part limited in time and space. He experiences himself, his thoughts, and feeling as something separated from the rest, a kind of optical delusion of his consciousness. This delusion is a kind of prison for us, restricting us to our personal desires and to affection for a few persons nearest to us. Our task must be to free ourselves from this prison by widening our circle of compassion to embrace all living creatures and the whole of nature in its beauty.

The power of interdependence comes from our profound understanding that our fates are inextricably linked. For those who hold a narrow and short-term view of the world would fail to see this to the detriment of all. The power of interdependence is that it naturally gives rise to kindness and consideration for others. Not because it is the right thing to do but because I am the other.

Meeting My Dark King

Like many women I know, I also have had several negative and hurtful sexual experiences in my life. In fact, days before leaving for my vision quest to the deserts of Arizona, I had an incident where my potential business partner was inappropriately fondling my hand and attempted to kiss me despite the fact that I explained to him that I was happily married and definitely not interested in him in a sexual way. I left the meeting feel angry and agitated.

I have also had spontaneous past-life visions of myself as a comfort woman, women conscripted by the Japanese army to serve in army-operated brothels. These women were either forcibly taken or tricked into believing that they are getting a job to support their families. There is no question that there has been a long history of abuse of women by men in the world that still continues to this day. It is easy to get angry at these injustices and feel, even in an unconscious way, anger and even rage against men.

My experience during my vision quest drastically changed my view. One night during my vision quest, I had a dream where I was being chased by seemingly evil zombie-like beings. The next day I was wandering through the desert and got a peculiar sensation that I was being chased by these beings again. It was broad daylight, so I had no reason to feel scared, but I could not shake off this eerie feeling. My steps quickened almost to a light jog until I heard in my head, "We are not here to hurt you, we are here to usher you to our king, your king."

That moment I stopped being scared and became curious. I decided to "follow" these invisible beings. I eventually ended up at a dried-up riverbed that was black from the silt left behind by the river. On either side of the river were tall rock cliffs that were also covered in the black silt and gave off the feeling that I was walking inside a dark fortress. I continued walking until I was stopped in my tracks by a huge boulder in the shape of a throne, large enough for two people. I intuitively knew that I had arrived at my destination. Here I was welcomed by my dark king, or as Carl Jung would say, my animus – my masculine inner personality. He was my inner lover, my other.

In him, I felt the savage violence that was perpetrated against women over millennia, but somehow, I understood that this was in me, part of me! I was the perpetrator and perpetrated all at once. He commanded me to strip naked. I obeyed without hesitation. Then I made love to him, to myself, leading to the most exquisite ecstatic orgasm. I felt like I was making love to nature, the sky, the wind, myself, and my inner lover, the dark king all at once. The unconscious grudge I held against men melted away and was replaced by a recognition of myself in them. I could not even call this emotion forgiveness as I was able to completely identify with the sufferings and story of the perpetrator that brought him to where he was. The power of interdependence allows you to see yourself as the other, which enables senseless emotions like jealousy, fear of rejection, and need for control to fade away.

In the Tibetan Buddhist traditions, female deities called *dakinis* are depicted with a long staff called *khavtanga* with vajra at its tip to represent the masculine, while male deities are shown with a staff with a trident at the end that represents the feminine. The *khavtanga* represents the inner consort of these deities. What these sacred images are sharing is that we must claim and own our inner consort to be whole and to elevate our consciousness beyond ego-based emotions like jealousy, insecurity, and a sense of not being enough. In the deserts of Arizona, I inadvertently encountered my *khavtanga*, my inner consort.

Story of the Redwood Forest

I have always been in awe of the majesty of the redwood forest in California. I always assumed that their roots would be just as deep and impressive as the massive height of their trunk and branches. So, I was very surprised to hear that their root system is quite shallow and they depend on each other for survival. Reading *The Secret Lives of Trees* by Peter Wohlleben gave me further insight into how trees communicated with each other. The story of the redwood forest is a perfect illustration of the power of interdependence. Each tree independently soars to unimaginable heights, yet without her sisters and brothers to support, protect, and nourish her, she would never even get past the sapling stage.

One of my clients once said to me, the ideal work force is 70% men and 30% women. I was surprised and asked her why she felt that way. She replied that she felt working with men was more efficient and found women too emotional. My client was a successful executive with a degree in law and accounting. Her masculine side was well developed, yet without the balance of her feminine aspect she had challenges in relationships both at work and romantically. Fortunately for her, she was able to get in touch with her feminine strength of interdependence, which resulted in her building a supportive and loyal team around her.

According to an Harvard Business Review article, "Defend Your Research: What Makes a Team Smarter? More Women,"[9] group intelligence increases when there are more women. In fact, the article goes so far as to say that the group intelligence of women is higher than that of groups of men. Individual intelligence was not different but when in a group, more women meant higher group intelligence. This is a clear indication of the power of interdependence as strongly feminine trait.

EXERCISE: Shamanic Tool for Resolving Conflict or Pacifying

When you are in conflict or stress, your perspective narrows, and it becomes difficult to see another point of view or come up with creative solutions. This exercise will help you take a step back and gain perspective as well as create an opportunity to shift things on an energetic level. You can use this tool to communicate on the quantum energetic level with another person, animal, or even a place. I have used this tool to successfully resolve conflict with my mother, prepare for an important work conference, and comfort a dog suffering from separation anxiety.

1. Take a deep breath in and as you exhale close your eyes.

2. Scan your body from head to toe, noticing any physical, emotional, or mental tension.

3. Bring your breath to that area as if you had pair of nostrils at the point of tension and, using the breath, let go of any tension. Exhale with your mouth open, making an audible sound of release.

4. Every time you breathe into the space, imagine the spot filling with light and, as you exhale, the tension in that area dissolving with your open-mouth exhales.

5. It is important to keep your mouth open for the exhale as this helps release tension and stagnant energy from the body.

6. When the tension in your body is released, bring your attention to your heart. Really feel the sensations in your heart. Shamans believe that the voice of the heart is the voice of the Universe.

7. Imagine a ball of light forming in your heart and then witness it rising through your body to top of your head.

8. The ball of energy is now hovering above your head. This, the energy ball, represents your higher self that is connected to Universal collective consciousness.

9. Now imagine the person you wish to communicate with in front of you. Look for the energy ball hovering above their head.

10. From the place of your higher self, communicate with the other's higher self.

11. It may be helpful to prepare some specific questions that are pertinent to the situation.

12. Once you are satisfied and the conversation complete, thank the other person for engaging in the conversation.

13. Witness the energy ball returning to your heart.

14. Open your eyes and journal what you have learned.

CHAPTER 12

Power of Nature

*Those who are inspired by a model
other than nature labor in vain.*

– Leonardo Da Vinci

I had been meditating seven days straight for ten hours each day starting at 4:30 a.m. The first three days were torturous. Every muscle in my body ached and my mind was flitting around like a wild bird trapped in a small cage. Somehow everything changed on the seventh day. My mind was still, like a lake on a windless day and luminescent like the sun reflecting on the calm surface of the water. During the short lunch break, I took a walk in the woods. One moment I was feeling the warmth of the sun on my skin and the next I felt my body diffuse and every single cell in my body transform to beams of light. In that state, everything around me looked and felt different. The trees, plants, the rocks, and wind came alive and were whispering to me. I understood then that everything around me is sentient and sacred.

The root word for solitude, *solitudo,* is Latin for nature. In solitude, away from everyday stimuli, you are able to remember yourself as the part of everything, as part of nature. And in this solitude and connection, you are able to rediscover ease, sensuality, belonging, and the deep wisdom within you. Solitude in nature allows you to shed light onto what brings you alive and what does not.

This is why I am dismayed when I meet women who hate to get a little dirt underneath their nails. Feminine wisdom is wild, animate, and unpredictable. Voluntarily imprisoned in our sterile concrete habitats, we have lost touch with the beauty and rhythms of nature. Women have succumbed to images presented by advertisers of what is attractive and beautiful, creating generations of women who are dolls, a product of social expectations, especially men and corporate propaganda.

Don't get me wrong, I absolutely love the artistry and creativity of the fashion industry and appreciate what a bit of well-applied makeup can do to my complexion.

However, this cannot compare to the innate beauty that is within us all. Sure, it can enhance it, but without connecting to this wild natural magnificence that is inherent in us, we are hollow shells.

Mother Earth as Teacher and Guide

History shows that patriarchy and industrialization go hand in hand. The masculine approach conquers and bends nature to his will while the feminine path, which was evident in older civilizations, honored, respected, and worked with nature.

Ecofeminists such as Françoise d'Eaubonne argue that there are evident connections between women and nature. She argues that the fate of all subordinate groups (women, people of color, children, the poor) consistently went hand in hand with that of nature. All of these subordinate groups have been subject to oppression, domination, exploitation, and colonization from a patriarchal society that also exploited nature as a commodity rather than viewed it as the source of life. Ecofeminists believe that the connection between women and nature are further illustrated through the fact that traditionally "feminine" values such as reciprocity, nurturing, and cooperation are present in both women and in nature.

Many cultures refer to our planet as *Mother Earth* or *Mother Nature*. Mother Earth is a true representation of feminine power. She can be nurturing, gentle, sustaining as well as unpredictable, fierce, and sometimes destructive. Yet, her sometimes devastating aspect always has a purpose, although as humans we are unable to comprehend it. To her, all life on this planet is her children, not just humans.

After years of attending various workshops offered by renowned teachers, I have reached the point of what economists call "diminishing return." Always being hungry to grow and evolve, I started to get a little depressed about my future spiritual path and that is when I heard clearly in my head, "Come to me, I shall be your teacher." It was Mother Earth speaking to me. In hindsight, she was with me throughout my journey all along.

We spoke of signs and synchronicities. This is how Mother Earth speaks to us and teaches us. Natural life around us can be the most profound teacher if you care to watch and listen. Einstein had said, *"Look deeply into nature and you will understand everything better."* Leonardo da Vinci was also known to have modeled many of his inventions after nature.

Understanding Signs from Nature

How do you know if you have received a sign? First, a deep question must have been asked. You may be thinking, "Well, I didn't really ask a question," but truth is many of us are often carrying around a deep question coming from our soul. You may not always be conscious of it. For example, you may be unhappy in your relationship or work and wondering if you should stay or leave. You may have not directed this question to Mother Earth, but if your question is sincere and heartfelt, she is probably already guiding you toward your inner knowing. Secondly, when you see a sign, there is very likely a strong emotional reaction.

One day, I noticed a huge wasp holding onto something and resting on my window screen. First, I was shocked by the size of the wasp. It was at least the length of my index finger. When I looked more closely, I realized that the object the wasp was grasping was a cicada. I was so intrigued by what I saw that I ran to get my camera, but by the time I came back it had flown away. The image of this huge wasp transporting the dead cicada intrigued me and I could not get it out of my mind. I felt it was a sign. At the time I was feeling really frustrated at work. It seemed that despite my diligent and organized attempts, things just weren't going the way I had hoped.

Upon contemplating the meaning of this sign, I questioned what the wasp meant to me. Wasps to me represented a single-minded quality of productivity and organization. It does not question what it is doing but rather assiduously plows away at its given task. Cicadas on the other hand remain underground for much of their lives before emerging to spend a brilliant summer singing until its end. The cicada represented patience followed by breaking free and letting my inner voice emerge.

The wasp had killed the cicada. My overly-planning nature did not leave room for creativity or mystery. I was trying to do everything instead of honoring that unknown creative force that is truly the source of all manifestation. I understood now why I was stuck. My limited ego had convinced me that I was responsible and if I really worked hard all will be well. Only when I recognized that I had crowded out the sacred in my life did things start moving again. In fact, when I let go of my "grasping" nature I was able to positively shift things in my life. *The Dalai Lama's wise words reflect the lesson the wasp and cicada taught me: "I am open to the guide of synchronicity and do not let expectations hinder my path."*

Freedom and Femininity

Enchanting femininity is not about lipstick and high heels, but rather a state of being relaxed with your natural self. Allowing yourself the freedom to be yourself is the key to embracing the feminine power within.

The first day I joined an ecstatic dance class, I was self-conscious, and my movements were pre-choreographed in my head. I took pride in my ability to keep a beat and I didn't want to look the fool. Usually when I danced, I was in high heels, a slinky outfit, and makeup. Today was different. I was barefoot in a simple tank top and a flowy bohemian skirt. Being manicured and refined seemed out of place. Many of the other dancers were not exactly graceful but there was a wild beauty about them that gave me pause.

I closed my eyes and let the music flow through me. At first, I hardly moved. It almost seemed like the music was penetrating my body one cell at a time. Eventually, all the cells in my body came alive and I started moving like I have never moved before. I felt such freedom that tears started streaming down my face. I felt sensual, exotic, and powerful. I was a goddess awakened by the pulsing music in my being.

In Tibetan Buddhist traditions, the divine feminine is depicted as a Dakini, a wild, naked dancing enlightened figure who is alluring and fearsome at once. In her book *Wisdom Rising: Journey into the Mandala of the Empowered Feminine*, Lama Tsultrim states:

> *Dakinis are the undomesticated female energies: spiritual, erotic, ecstatic and wise, playful and profound, fierce and peaceful that are beyond the grasps of the conceptual mind. There is a place for our whole feminine being, in all its guises, to be present.*

Lama Tsultrim explains that the infinite and wild natural feminine transcends ideas of pure and impure, clean and unclean. She cuts through notions of duality and enables you to view all life as sacred. This perception of non-duality gives you freedom from the shackles of self-imposed rigidity of perfectionism, and this is your true state as Mother Nature intended.

Embracing the Power of Nature Within

During an all-night shamanic meditation working with sacred plants, I was able to gain insight into honoring and embracing my own true nature. Right before dawn, the shaman who was leading the session introduced us to a simple tune. Anyone who wanted to share their voice could simply raise their voice and lead the group. At this moment an inner vision of a black panther appeared to me.

She is my power animal and had appeared many times in my visions, so normally I feel happy to see her. However, this time was different. She peered at me from the dark. I felt scared. I was afraid of my own power animal, who normally protects and guides me in my visions. In a flash of insight, I realized I was afraid of my own personal power and also was rejecting my true nature. She leapt at me as I became aware of this and ripped my throat open. I saw myself dying, bleeding on the ground. This was what the shamans and healers would refer to as death of the ego.

Like the variety of species of plants and animals who all live according to their true nature, we also have an essence that is unique to us. Misguided by social expectations, I realized I was trying to be someone I was not and this was causing considerable tension and stress in me. I am a shadow cat, whose nature is to be a formidable force behind the scenes. It was not in my nature to be overt and be in the spotlight, yet this is what I thought I needed to do to succeed.

As I watched my ego-self bleeding and dying on the ground, I spontaneously started singing. The deep resonance of my voice surprised myself and even my husband, who later told me he didn't recognize my voice. Understanding my true nature and embracing it fully gave me the inner confidence and aligned integrity to raise my voice and sing my heart song in a way I never had before.

Later I came across the personal branding system called *The Fascinate Advantage*[10]. Upon completing the assessment, the insight I gained from my vision was confirmed. How I was expressing myself was not congruent with who I truly was and it was leading to inner conflict, stress, and procrastination. Needless to say, after this validation, I drastically shifted my voice and personal brand.

EXERCISE: Communing with Mother Nature

There is almost nothing I love more than being in nature. Every chance I get, I find a way to get deep in nature where I can no longer hear the cacophony of modern civilization. To deepen your experience with nature, it is helpful to create a conscious ritual for the encounter.

One important tip is to use your imagination and have fun. Einstein said that logic can get you from A to Z, but imagination can get you anywhere. Imagination is a gateway to your intuitive abilities. It is the Universal Consciousness speaking to you. Do not dismiss, degrade, or belittle your imagination. I often hear clients say, "Oh, I feel like I just made it up" or "It's just my imagination." But ask yourself, where does this imagination come from? Certainly not logic! Imagination helps you get out of your usual way of thinking and get us out of our limiting and restricting box. So truly honor your imagination for this exercise.

The Universe speaks to us in metaphors and your imagination is the key to unlocking these signs.

1. Find a spot in nature as far away from civilization as you dare to go.

2. If possible, get to the spot before or around dawn and expect to return at dusk.

3. It is best to do this solo, so you will have no other distractions.

4. At the beginning of the journey, pick a marker that signals the boundary between your ordinary world and the magical and mysterious world of nature. This can be two trees or two rocks or any other natural landmarks.

5. If you can't find suitable markers, you can create your own with rocks or tree branches. You will enter into the extraordinary world of nature and leave behind your ordinary world the moment you step through this gate. You will also return to your ordinary world through this gate.

6. Right in front of the gate, close your eyes and take a deep breath. As you exhale, step into the magical world of nature.

7. Once you are on this side of the gate, everything that you take notice of is a message from Mother Nature. Not all of them will be earth-shattering epiphanies, some of it may seem like gentle chatter with a friend.

8. Let yourself be guided by Mother Nature with no specific path in mind.

9. It may be helpful to also employ the Soft Vision exercise from Chapter 8 to further heighten your ability to perceive and hear.

10. Take time to journal your insights throughout the day.

11. Return to the gate you created at the beginning of your journey. Before your step through, offer a bow to Mother Nature for her insights and then step back to your ordinary life, enriched by your time in nature.

CHAPTER 13

Power of Embodiment

Embodiment is a curious word. Dictionaries define it as *"to provide with a body or make corporeal or even to collect into a body."* Inherent in the word is the concept of a non-corporal form taking on physical form. Aside from the concept of the soul, there is certainly a part of that which we call consciousness (i.e. mind) separate from the sensations of the body. All the joys, sorrows, pleasure, and pain of life happen because we have a body. In many spiritual and religious traditions, the body and its desires are considered dirty and impure. This also is a byproduct of patriarchal civilization that either felt threatened by or didn't appreciate the feminine. The exile of Lilith from the Garden of Eden is a metaphor for this unfortunate development.

Alexa was a voluptuous Persian woman who was naturally sensual and feminine, but she struggled with low self-esteem and was constantly in and out of unhealthy relationships. Working with her, I was able to uncover her belief that the body was sinful and not to be trusted. Instinct and intuition come from the body. While your conscious mind can only hold a certain amount of information, your body is recording and responding to millions of stimuli every second and this makes the body a powerful tool to make good decisions. Since Alexa believed her body to be dirty and untrustworthy, it is no wonder that she made poor decisions when it came to men and was constantly attracted to men who treated her the way she felt about her body.

In this chapter, we will explore how the power of embodiment can create presence, sensuality, and even provide a path to personal and spiritual growth.

Source of Presence

This may be a strange concept for some, but in this fast-paced modern society your consciousness is often not in your body. Unlike the body, your mind is not limited by time and space. You can be dreaming of the future or living in the past and creating emotions in your body in the current moment from the thoughts in your mind for the future and past.

The barrage of external stimuli that we face day to day also pulls you out of your body. Social media, Netflix binging, hours in front of computers at work, all take us out of the moment and start creating *energy in motions* that are not truly yours. This leads to depression, apathy, and anxiety as you are letting external stimuli constantly dictate your energy state.

The body, on other hand, is anchored to the present moment and this is why the body is the perfect tool to cultivate presence. All negativity stems from not being present. Anxiety, tension, stress, and worry are all forms of fear caused by your mind being in the future. Whereas guilt, regret, shame, bitterness, anger, and resentment are caused by the mind being in the past.

The present moment is all we have. There is nothing we can do about the past or the future, so ruminating in these non-present times is a waste of energy – and I mean that quite literally. You are actually wasting energy from your body to consume yourself with thoughts of the past or future. Starting from a neutral state, try to imagine an incident that depressed you from the past. Stay with the experience for a while and observe how your energy shifts. You will most likely start to feel heavy and unmotivated. Thoughts literally consume your energy reserve. Taoist and yogic traditions knew this and hence presence through embodiment was a main focus of their practices.

Embodiment is the key to presence and presence is the key to mindfully creating the life you want. Then, how do we become present? It's very simple. Feel your body. The first meditation taught by the Buddha to his students was a meditation of presence through scanning the body from head to toe, over and over again. During this meditation of simply feeling the body, many emotions and aches and pains arise as memory is stored in every cell of the body.

Being deeply embodied, that is, present in the body, you are able to proactively affect your energy field and positively shift your present life toward that of your dreams. If you continue to ruminate in the past and future, you will be leaving your body and your life an empty shell vulnerable to invasion of ghosts of past and future that drain your energy.

Are you always feeling rushed and your mind is always on the next thing? This is because you live in the illusion that it is solely your actions that manifest the things you desire. The truth is it is mostly our energy that manifests, and when your consciousness is not in the body and in the present the misalignment of mind-body makes us lose our power to influence the present moment, which is the only thing that is real and only time we can manifest.

Source of Sensuality

Allison was a beautiful woman to behold but there was an awkward rigidity about her that made her less appealing.

When she came to my office, I asked her to stand up, close her eyes, and shake off the stress of the day by bouncing her knees gently. When she attempted to follow my instructions, she jerked up and down almost robotically as if she was a stranger to her body. She could not feel a rhythm in her movement and there was certainly no gracefulness or fluidity.

Highly intelligent people who are primarily head-brain led tend to be awkward in their body. Think of the stereotype of a science or computer geek. The minds of these highly mental people are indeed lost to whatever latest formula they are working on. The same goes for many business executives. Their minds are often preoccupied with work even during non-working hours.

Sensuality is one of the most alluring and enchanting qualities of a woman and it is accessed through embodiment. Sensuality requires you to be fully present in your body and with intimate knowledge of your own body. Throughout our lives we spend hours at school and work cultivating and honing mental skills; in contrast, how much time have you spent being in your body reveling in the sensations your body offers?

So many women suffer from poor body image, which severs them from their natural sensuality. I have read the sad statistic that 91% of American women are unhappy with their bodies. Poor body image leads to low self-esteem, which often leads to engaging in unhealthy relationships and even suicide. Furthermore, 95% of women with eating disorders are aged 12-25![11] We can continue to blame the media for its unrealistic portrayal of women but truly the ability to change things lies in us. It is time to stop exploiting your body as if it were some status symbol and accept your body just as-is, for what it is, the sacred house of your soul and the vehicle for life experiences in all its sensuality.

Receptivity and Sensuality

The senses and embodiment are inextricable tied. When you are fully embodied, your senses come alive and in this state you are fully receptive. Obvious as it may seem, without being receptive to the stimuli of the senses, you cannot experience sensuality. You may be wondering, well, how could you possibly ignore the obvious stimulation of the senses? But it happens all the time. The brain has an amazing ability to divert our attention at the expense of embodiment. Have you ever laid in bed while your lover was trying to seduce or make love to you and all you can think of is your work day and you can't really feel any pleasure from what he is doing? In fact, you may be even thinking, *can we just get this over with so I can go to bed?*

Many high-achieving women are very heady. Their mental capacities become a huge handicap when it comes to embodiment and sensuality. Receptivity is at the core of femininity, sensuality, and embodiment.

Map of Transformation in the Body

Unlike common religious views of disparaging the body as sinful or of base animal nature, ancient sages have known that the body holds the map to enlightenment. It is important to understand that your body actually holds the key to reaching your highest potential.

Below is a diagram of the energy centers in the body, also known as *chakras*. Remember, emotions are energy in motion and these energy centers each resonate and hold different emotional aspects. They are also related to specific organs in our endocrine system that are responsible for hormones in our body as well as psychological developmental stages.

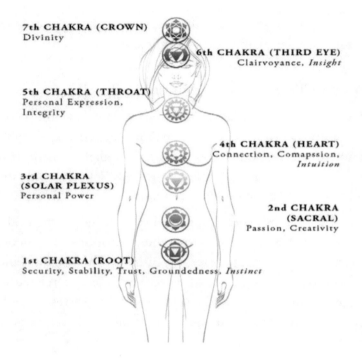

Figure 4 Chakra System

From the bottom up, the first chakra is the root chakra. It is the gate through which our physical body enters this world. It corresponds to your time in your mother's womb to twelve months of age. During this time, you are completely dependent on your mother or a caretaker. According to Eriksonian developmental maps, it is no surprise you learn the concepts of trust vs. mistrust during this stage. Strong foundation in the root chakra means that you have a healthy and stable view of the world around you, neither excessively fearful nor naively trusting. In my Seven Element System this chakra corresponds to the nurturing earth element.

The second chakra, or sacral chakra, corresponds to the ages of six months to two years old. Its position is in the middle of the womb (or a similar spot in the body if you are a man). The second chakra is where the qualities of creativity, pleasure, attraction, and passion reside. This energy center is called the Lower Palace by Taoists and is the physical energy center of your body. Low energy in this chakra results in the lack of energy to magnetize or manifest our desired outcomes. In the Seven Element System, it is associated with the dynamic fire element.

The third chakra, or solar plexus, corresponds to the ages of eighteen months to four years and during this time your favorite word is "no!" It is a time in which toddlers exert their own independence. The third chakra holds the energy for you to exert your personal power. Imbalance in this chakra is expressed either as a controlling megalomaniac or a withdrawn self-effacing doormat. Both expressions are caused by an instability in the third chakra. In the Seven Element System, this is associated with the sharp and resilient metal element.

The fourth chakra, or the heart chakra, corresponds to social connections and corresponds to three to seven years in age. Children during this age transition from parallel play to interactive play as they become more interested in interaction and connecting to their peers. The fourth chakra is the seat of our intuition and heart intelligence. It affects how you emotionally relate to others and yourself. Most animals have the previous three chakras as these energy centers hold instinctive qualities of survival, pleasure/pain, and control. The fourth chakra is where the non-instinctive human qualities start to develop. This is the seat of qualities like compassion and unconditional love. When this chakra is depleted, you are generally withdrawn and shutdown or excessively emotional, clingy and needy. Compassion arising from an open heart chakra is naturally expansive as it comes from transcending the limiting view of me and other. Taoists call this the Middle Palace and it is the source of emotional maturity. In the Seven Element System, this is associated with the generous wood element.

The fifth chakra corresponds to ages seven to twelve years old and a time where you are starting to explore social contracts and expectations versus your view of self and how to bring themselves into alignment between the two.

This chakra is positioned in your throat and is all about self-expression and how you show up in the world. When you feel grounded and safe (first chakra); passionate about life (second chakra); have healthy self-esteem and willpower (third chakra); and feel genuine connection and empathy to those around you (fourth chakra), expressing yourself is joyful and matter of fact. Your need to be heard is met. However, blockages in any of the first four chakras affect your ability speak up and show up in the world leading to a sense of insignificance. In the Seven Element System, this is associated with the levity of the air element.

The sixth chakra, also known as the third eye, is developmentally associated with adolescence. In this threshold into adulthood, adolescence is a time where your perception of the world is shaped. With solid foundations from the first to the fifth chakras, clear vision without distortion is achieved. The place of the sixth chakra is in the middle of your brain where your pineal gland is. Out of balance, you are delusional, obsessive, insensitive, and in denial as you are unable to see what is truly going on. In balance, you are imaginative, perceptive, and insightful. Taoists call this the Upper Palace, where luminous divinity can be cultivated. In the Seven Element System, this is associated with the deep wisdom of the water element.

The seventh chakra corresponds to adulthood. This is the time where you consider your contribution and significance in the world, as well as your place in it. Your relation to the divine (or some larger force beyond yourself) is explored during this period. When out of balance, your belief systems are rigid and you tend to be cynical and apathetic or, on the flip side, you may indulge in spiritual escapism and disassociate with your body. When in balance, you are able to have a higher perspective and assimilate and integrate information in a healthy way. You are open-minded, curious, and humble. This is the transcendent spirit element in the Seven Element System.

Traumas during any of the developmental stages are trapped in the body and recorded in your chakras, affecting all subsequent chakras. The energy centers in the body provide a diagnostic tool as well as a map for healing and growth. The answers we seek, the medicines to heal, and tools to grow are all within your body.

EXERCISE: Chakra Balancing

This sound meditation utilizes the seed syllables that convey the nature of each chakra to purify and balance your chakras.

1. Sit in a comfortable lotus, half-lotus, or cross-legged position. I highly recommend sitting on a cushion so that you can keep your back straight without straining.

2. Close your eyes to bring your attention inward.

3. Take a few deep breaths.

4. Visualize a sunrise that will start from the bottom of your seat. As you say the sound syllable for each chakra, you will witness the sun rising.

5. Bring your attention to your first chakra near your tailbone and say the word Lam. Feel the vibration created in your first chakra. Repeat 3–5 more times.

6. Bring your attention to your second chakra, in the middle of your womb, and say the word, Vam. Feel the vibrations created by the sound in your womb. Repeat 3–5 more times.

7. Bring your attention to your third chakra, your solar plexus and say the word, Ram. Feel the vibrations created by the sound in stomach. Repeat 3–5 more times.

8. Bring your attention to your fourth chakra, in the middle of your sternum, and say the word, Yam. Feel the vibrations created by the sound in your sternum and heart. Repeat a few more times.

9. Bring your attention to your fifth chakra, in the middle of your throat, and say the word, Ham. Feel the vibrations created by the sound in your throat. Repeat a few more times.

10. Bring your attention to your sixth chakra, in the middle of your brain, and say the word, Om. Feel the vibrations created by the sound in your head. Feel the sound filling and expanding from the middle of your brain to your whole brain and head, then up to the top of your head, your crown. Repeat a few more times.

11. Take a few deep breaths and open your eyes when you are ready.

CHAPTER 14

The Feminine Path

I have hereto outlined a number of feminine qualities, their associated powers, and how to cultivate them and apply to them to your daily life.

It is high time to embrace and integrate the magic, mystery, and power of the feminine path into your life. I do not say this from a "feminist" point of view. In fact, I feel many feminists are hardly feminine nor do they understand or appreciate basic concepts of femininity. I speak from the point of view of a humanist who believes that the integration of the feminine path is crucial for the wellbeing, and perhaps even the survival, of our species. Here is an excerpt from John Perkins, a former energy industrialist who turned to one of the forerunners of cogeneration initiatives and a staunch supporter of indigenous cultures, their people and their way of life[12]:

> *"The colonists developed an alternative form of government. As a model they turned once again to the Indians, especially the Iroquois, a nation composed of five, and later six, tribes. Many of the Founding Fathers of the United States – men like Benjamin Franklin, Thomas Jefferson, George Washington, Thomas Paine – visited indigenous communities in order to better understand their ways. Based on their studies, they arrived at a system of government that has been copied all over the world."*

> *"I hadn't heard that about the Iroquois."*

> *"Yes, but the Founding Fathers neglected one thing. Among the Iroquois, it was a council of women who chose tribal chiefs. In essence, the women elected the captain, a man, to steer the ship. If they didn't like the course he charted, they replaced him. Our Founding Fathers failed to include the women. They didn't allow women the right to vote at all – until this century, over one hundred years after the Constitution was written."*

> *"The most significant – most disastrous – shapeshift in human history.*

> *Voting?" He laughed.*

"Of course not. The shift away from the feminine. This world is basically feminine, you know. It's what allows survival. Not 'survival of the fittest' – that's just a male concept. Survival is all about nurturing, loving, sustaining – the feminine aspects. Without them, where would we be? Our early history was predominantly one that honored these qualities; like your Iroquois, women decided all the important issues. My culture here worshiped the goddess, as did people all over the world – all over Mother Earth – until recent history, a few thousand years ago, perhaps a couple of thousand years before Christ. Then a great and terrible shapeshift took place.... Our ugly shadow is not only for inner feminine that has been neglected and imprisoned but is also betrayal of Mother Earth."

Honoring and embracing your feminine powers is a mission that has far-reaching consequences beyond your ability to be more alluring to a potential lover or magnetize the things we want in life. On a level of epigenetics, we are responsible for shifting the attitude toward the feminine for future generations, and on the level of the world we are responsible for what is happening to Mother Earth. But it all starts with you. Your ability to embrace, rejoice, and hold your femininity sacred.

References

1. https://verilymag.com/2016/05/oxytocin-sex-
    differences-women-hormones-bonding-sex-trust

    https://www.livescience.com/42198-what-is-oxytocin.html

2. Sfirah is singular form of Sfirot. According to Kabbalah,
    Sfirot are emanations of the limitless primordial creative
    force, which are expressed in 10 attributes that manifest
    the physical and metaphysical realms.

3. www.chabad.org/parshah/article_cdo/aid/399291/
    jewish/The-Female-Estate.htm

    http://ascentofsafed.com/cgi-bin/ascent.
    cgi?Name=feminine

4. Manuela Dunn Mascetti and Peter Lorie,
    Nostradamus: Prophecies for Women, Simon &
    Schuster, 1995, p. 47.

5. Body Image Stats: https://www.statisticbrain.com/body-image-statistics/ Medication Stats: https://www.cdc.gov/nchs/data/hus/hus16.pdf#079

6. The User Illusion Book

7. https://www.wimhofmethod.com/

8. The unconscious perception of movement and spatial orientation arising from stimuli within the body itself. This ability is sometimes considered to be your sixth sense.

9. https://hbr.org/2011/06/defend-your-research-what-makes-a-team-smarter-more-women

10. https://www.howtofascinate.com/

11. https://www.dosomething.org/us/facts/11-facts-about-body-image

12. Perkins, John. Shapeshifting: Techniques for Global and Personal Transformation (pp. 40-41). Inner Traditions/Bear & Company. Kindle Edition.

Acknowledgements

I am grateful to so many people who have been part of writing this book and supporting my work. To my publisher and mentor Angela Lauria and her team, I extend my deepest gratitude for bringing this book into fruition. I would like to express special thanks to Bethany Davis, my editor, for her genuine passion for this book and her keen eye, her refined talent to evolve this book and her warm caring spirit. I was heartened to see her first reaction when she read my book as I could feel that she was sincerely excited and touched by the manuscript. To my teacher Lama Tsultrim, I am grateful for her support of my work by writing the foreword to my book. I am also deeply honored to have her radiant presence in my life and to guide my spiritual journey. To my husband, who holds space for my growth and evolution with kindness and patience. I feel so lucky to have his love and solid presence in my life. To my dear friend and soul sisters Jen Sherer and Joana Vargas who have always believed in me and supported my various endeavors. Finally, to my readers and clients who have given me the opportunity to share my gifts, a big THANK YOU...

About the Author

Suki is a feminine leadership and relationship coach, author, and intuitive healer. Her passion is to empower women to embrace their divine femininity to create a new paradigm for feminine leadership.

Suki's journey into personal transformation started over a decade ago when her divorce left her physically and emotionally depleted. As work stress mounted, she found herself with chronic back pain, insomnia, migraines, and depression that made her determined to regain her emotional and physical health. When MRIs, CT scans, and western medical approaches did not provide satisfactory long-term answers or solutions, she looked to holistic mind-body-spirit approaches.

This led her to study many esoteric and spiritual paths. The exploration of these various paths led to her deep appreciation and fascination of the subtle energies that influence our daily lives. Through various energy modalities, Suki helps clients reclaim their awareness and connection to the Universal energy to optimize mental and physical health.

A central piece of her work is to assist her clients to reclaim and cultivate divine feminine aspects of fluidity, heart-centeredness, and intuition. So many women in the work force have lost touch of their feminine super powers as they modeled men to become successful in their careers. Suki shares a vision and process to help women develop a new leadership paradigm for women.

Previously, Suki worked in finance and media with Fortune 100 companies such as the Walt Disney Company, News Corporation, Lehman Brothers, and Fortress Investment Group. She has a B.A. in History from Bryn Mawr College and MBA from INSEAD, France. She lives in Irvington, New York with her husband John O'Connor and her two sons.

Thank You!

Thank you for reading *Alpha Bitch to Enchantress*. I hope you found some useful insights and tools to awaken your feminine super powers.

I have provided a Femininity Quotient ("FQ") Assessment Tool in my book but would like to offer a little gift for those who are really ready to take the next step. I am providing a personalized FQ Report and you can get yours by visiting my website at: www.sukisohn.com/femininity-quotient

You will also be able to download guided meditations and links to the Spotify Playlists for the movement practices suggested in the book at www.sukisohn.com/resources.

OTHER BOOKS FROM SUKI:

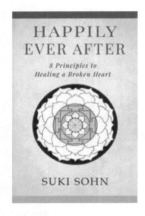

Happily Ever After

8 Principles for Healing a Broken Heart